The Spirit of Africville

SECOND EDITION

SELECTED AND EDITED BY THE AFRICVILLE GENEALOGY SOCIETY

WITH CONTRIBUTIONS BY DONALD CLAIRMONT, STEPHEN KIMBER, BRIDGLAL PACHAI AND CHARLES SAUNDERS

FORMAC PUBLISHING COMPANY LIMITED
HALIFAX

Formac Publishing Company Limited recognizes the support of the Province of Nova Scotia through the Department of Tourism, Culture and Heritage. We acknowledge the financial support of the Government of Canada through the Canada Book Fund for our publishing activities. Formac Publishing Company Limited acknowledges the support of the Canada Council for the Arts for our publishing program.

Library and Archives Canada Cataloguing in Publication

The spirit of Africville / with contributions by Donald Clairmont ... [et al.].—2nd ed.

Issued also in electronic format.
ISBN 978-0-88780-925-5

1. Africville (Halifax, N.S.)—History. 2. Africville (Halifax, N.S.)—Pictorial works. 3. Black Canadians—Nova Scotia—Halifax—Social conditions. I. Clairmont, Donald H. (Donald Hayden), 1938-

FC2346.9.B6S65 2010   971.6'22500496   C2010-902676-4

Formac Publishing Company Limited
5502 Atlantic Street
Halifax, Nova Scotia, Canada
B3H 1G4
www.formac.ca

Printed and bound in Hong Kong

TABLE OF CONTENTS

ACKNOWLEDGEMENTS

This book is an outgrowth of the exhibition "Africville: A Spirit that Lives On," and a related conference held at the Mount Saint Vincent Art Gallery.

These events were generated by the Africville Exhibition Steering Committee whose members were: Irvine Carvery, President, Africville Genealogy Society; Henry Bishop, Curator, Black Cultural Centre for Nova Scotia; Bridglal Pachai, then Director of the Black Cultural Centre and now Executive Director of the Nova Scotia Human Rights Commission; Shelagh Mackenzie, Producer, the National Film Board, Atlantic Centre; and Mary Sparling, Director, Art Gallery, Mount Saint Vincent University.

Throughout, the steering committee consulted extensively with Donald Clairmont, Department of Sociology, Dalhousie University.

The committee would also like to acknowledge the valuable assistance received from Bernard Hart, Director, Education Media Services, Nova Scotia Department of Education.

The exhibition and its national tour were funded by the Museums Assistance Program of the federal Department of Communications.

The members of the Genealogy Society Book Committee are: Ray and Eve Lawrence; the Touisaint Family — Carol, Jim, Carrie and Joanne; Rod Dixon; Nelson Carvery; Linda Mantley; George Grant Jr.; Stan and Alice Carvery; Brenda Steed-Ross.

Royalties from the sale of the book are going to the Africville Genealogy Society.

DEDICATION

This book is dedicated to the memory of Deborah Dixon-Jones, who left us December 7 1989. Deborah had three main objectives in her life, which were:

1 Playing an active role in the community where she could best serve

2 Expressing respect for the elders, seeking their knowledge and looking to them for guidance

3 Bestowing upon the youth an understanding of the importance of education and awareness about their culture

Pursuing these three objectives, Deborah became the main founder of the Africville Genealogy Society, which deals with the past, present and future affairs of the former residents of Africville, as she intended. She left behind this legacy to us.

Love
Linda Mantley, co-founder
Brenda Steed-Ross, co-founder

The beating heart of Africville was Seaview Church, place for Sunday school classes, pictured here.

PREFACE

We are Africville.

We are the little children who lie in the grass back the field daydreaming as clouds dance overhead.

We are Africville.

We are the little children who hears "blind" Howie Byers call out, "Com'ere one of you little children, I want you to go to the store for me."

We are Africville.

We are the little children who wakes up on an early Saturday morning to the smell of cardboard burning as Whoppie Sparks burns the boxes from his store.

We are Africville.

We are the little children who sits quietly in church while the congregation sings and sways to the spirit of an old spiritual.

We are Africville.

We are the little children who fall to sleep to the sounds of the whistle and beat of the 9 o'clock freight train moving through the village.

We are Africville.

We are the little children who feels the wind against their faces as we speed down Aunt Noggie's hill on sleds.

We are Africville.

We are the little children who takes their first dives into the water from the big rock down Kildare's Field.

We are Africville.

We are the little children who sit in Grandmother's sun porch listening to Great-Grandfather tell of life in Africville when he was a young boy.

We are Africville.

We are grown adults with little children of our own who will never share in the things and places we have known.

We are Africville.

As you read through the following pages of this book, remember the true spirit of Africville was in its people, not the quality of buildings or roads.

This book came out of a very important cultural event for the people of Africville. In conjunction with the Art Gallery, Mount St. Vincent University, the National Film Board, Atlantic Centre and the Black Cultural Centre, we put together an Art and Cultural Exhibit on the life and times of our community.

At the opening of the exhibit, a conference was held at the Mount that brought together the key people who were involved in the decision making process for the relocation to ask "Why?"

The people of Africville were there to describe life in Africville and how they felt then about the relocation, and how they feel now.

These discussions are captured in Chapter 4 of this book. Other chapters discuss the sociological perspective of Africville and the relocation, a walking tour through the community, and the story of the arrival of black settlers in Nova Scotia.

We, the people of Africville, hope that you will enjoy reading this book and gain a better understanding of what it is like to grow up in a black community in Nova Scotia.

Irvine Carvery
President, Africville Genealogy Society

CHAPTER 1

A VISIT TO AFRICVILLE

CHARLES SAUNDERS (WITH THE HELP OF OTHERS)

Summer, 1959

We start at the end of Barrington Street. See where the pavement cuts off and the dirt road beings? That's the "Welcome to Africville" sign. We're still on Barrington Street, you understand. But it's also the old Campbell Road, and it's got a history that goes way, way back in time.

Just call it "The Road." Everybody around here'll know what you're talkin' about.

You can still catch a little whiff of the oil the City sprays to lay the dust. If you look over to your right, you can see the docks of Pier 9. Some of our people work as stevedores down there, and on other docks all over the waterfront. You've got a good view of Bedford Basin from up here.

But wait till we get closer to the water. You'll really see something then.

Now we're crossing the first of the railroad tracks that pass through Africville. We call it the High Track, because of the way it slopes upward, like some kind of ski hill. But you ain't seen all the tracks yet. Farther down the road, we got a set of three. They slash through our community like a big pirate's sword. You don't think they had to tear down some houses to put those tracks in? No way to tell which side of *these* tracks is the right one or the wrong one — you know?

You better believe we learn about trains at a young

Left: Backyard garden view of Africville.
Opposite: An aerial view of Africville that shows its location on Bedford Basin, with north end Halifax and the Narrows in the background.

Above: Houses in Africville at its peak.
Opposite: Irma Sparks, a young musician.

age here. Trains are a big part of our lives. They can make some noise barrelin' through in the middle of the night! When they had steam locomotives, you used to be able to catch rides on the freight cars. Trains got a rhythm all their own. If you can catch the rhythm, you can catch the train.

We used to get coal that fell off the hoppers and the tender. In the wintertime, you need every piece of coal you can get to heat your house. No more of that, with these growlin' diesel engines. Steam engines sounded friendly; these diesels sound like they want to kill you. And they go too doggone fast.

Can't complain too much about the trains, though. Plenty of our menfolk worked as pullman porters. Travelled all over Canada and down in the States, they did. Kept those sleepin' cars cleaner than the Sheraton Hotel. They'd come home in their uniforms with the shiny brass buttons and they'd be like heroes comin' back from a war. Best job a coloured man could get back in the old days. Not so bad now either, if you want to know the truth.

Water, tracks and bushes — that's all you can see right now. Kind of reminds you of the country, even though we're still in Halifax. But you want to see some

houses, right? We've walked farther than Jesse Owens ever ran, and you're wonderin' when you're gonna see Africville.

Well, take a look up that hill past the tracks. See those houses up there, lookin' like raisins on a layer cake? That's the first part of Africville, if you're comin' in from Barrington Street. We call it Big Town. Don't know why; it ain't even the biggest part of Africville.

You want to know who lives there? The Byers family, the Carters, the Flints, and the Browns. Pay attention to those names, now. You'll be hearin' them again as we go along. Some of our names have a history goin' back to before there ever was an Africville. The first family to settle there was named Brown.

You probably heard of Queenie Byers. She does some bootleggin'. But don't get the idea that everybody here is a bootlegger. It's just another way to get by, that's all. The way some people talk, you'd think Africville was the only place that's got bootleggers.

We do have our fun, though. All kinds of parties. Remember when the soldiers and sailors came back after World War Two ended? It was one big party then! If you had a uniform on, you had it made in the shade.

Didn't need a phonograph to get a party goin'. Had plenty of musicians here just as good as what you hear on records. Boysie Dixon could make a piano sing like a bird in the sky. Archie Dixon played the saxophone and clarinet. We have guitar players, fiddlers, and drummers, too. Some folks even make their own instruments. Flutes carved from a tree branch, spoons, washboards — anything and everything. We have people that can sing some, too. You can get a whole concert goin' at the drop of a hat.

Kids playing on Bedford Basin.

Why, we even have some of our people study at the Halifax Conservatory of Music. Ruth Johnson — her name was Brown then — went there. So did Jessie Kane. And Ida Mae Thomas went down to Chicago and ended up playin' the organ for the biggest coloured church in the city.

Now, everybody wants to be Little Richard. That's him on the radio now. They sure don't teach *that* kind of music at the Conservatory. You can have a good time to it, though. Yes, indeed.

Maybe we'll pay visit up to Big Town on our way back. Bound to be somethin' goin' on. For now, though, let's just keep goin' up The Road.

Look over toward the water. See the big field there? We call that Kildare's Field. It's a good place for picnics. It's also a good place to go swimmin'. Look at those kids divin' off that big rock out in the water. They've probably been there since sunrise. And they'll still be there when the sun goes down.

This field's got some history. Used to be a bone mill here. A lot of our people worked there, makin' fertilizer. Then the mill shut down, and you can see what's left. Tell you somethin' else. Gypsies come to Kildare's Field every year. They pull up their wagons and stay for

Above: Rita Skinner on High Track.
Right: Walking up from Bedford Basin.

about a week or so, tellin' fortunes and all.

You can see the road slant downhill now. If you look up toward Big Town, you can't see the houses anymore. Those three tracks are almost like the High Track — up on a slope. This whole area's like a big scoop leading to the Basin.

And now that we're past Kildare's Field, we can see Joe and Retha Skinner's house. It's the first house you get to in Up The Road, or "Africville proper," or whatever you want to call it. You could say this is the "main part" of Africville, if you like to classify things.

Joe's out there bringin' up some water from his well. That's all the water we got here — wells. City says there's too much rock here to put in water lines. Don't make sense — we pay our taxes just like everybody else, but we had to petition the City for telephones and electricity. Ended up gettin' those things. But when we petition for water and sewers, all of a sudden

Looking into Tibby Alcock's yard.

the City goes deaf.

Hi, Joe. How you doin'? No, we're just passin' through right now. Maybe we'll drop by later.

We got to be careful about makin' too many commitments to go to people's houses. When you go to somebody's house in Africville, they're gonna offer you somethin' to eat. And you know better than to turn them down. We got to watch ourselves, or we'll be goin' out of here lookin' like prize pigs.

Speaking of pigs, people out here used to raise 'em. For a long time, there was a slaughterhouse on our outskirts. Once the slaughterhouse shut down, there wasn't no more reason to keep pigs.

Out behind Joe's house you can see Tibby's Pond. It's a tidal pond — you know. When the tide's out, there's a land bridge between the pond and the Basin. When the tide's in, it's all just part of the Basin. It's called Tibby's Pond because it's on Aunt Tibby Alcock's property.

Whose aunt is she? Well, everybody's. All the older folks here are Aunt or Uncle, Ma or Pa, whether they're related to you by blood or not. It's really like a big family out here. And you know what families are like — lovin' and fightin' all at the same time. Easy to get into, and hard to get out of.

Tibby's Pond is where our fishin' boats tie up. All kinds of fishin' goin' on here. Cod, mackerel, halibut, haddock, pollock — we catch all those different fish, just like everybody else in the Maritimes. We get crabs, mussels, and lobsters, too. Imagine poor people eatin' so many lobsters they get sick of 'em! Of course, the fishin' we do is what they call "non-commercial." All that means is, we eat what we catch.

Sometimes you can sell your fish down at the markets on the wharf. But some of the buyers start actin'

14

peculiar when they find out who did the catchin'. God bless 'em.

Next door to Aunt Tibby's is Deacon Ralph Jones's house. His son's house is right beside it. A lot of people build their houses on their parents' property. Keeps the land in the family, deed or no deed.

You can't miss the end of Deacon Jones's lot. That huge tree we're passing is about the biggest property marker you'll ever see. We call it the Caterpillar Tree. That's the only kind of fruit it grows — caterpillars. There's a story behind that tree. A long time ago, Deacon Jones went out and got a post to mark off his land. Next thing he knew, that post was sproutin' leaves, and over the years, it grew — and grew. Nobody knows why the caterpillars like it so much.

The Road's startin' to rise again now. See that ocean view? You couldn't buy a better view than that. When the wind's not blowin', the Basin looks like a sheet of glass. Maybe that's why there's so many houses here. Go ahead, wave to the people; you're among friends.

There's more Browns on this part of the road. There's also Clarence Carvery's place, and Mrs. MacDonald's. Yeah, there's MacDonalds here. What you think, they're all in Cape Breton?

You're noticin' the different colours people paint their houses. Like flowers, right? Folks do what they want to with their houses. If you want to have a different-lookin' door or window, that's OK. Keeps things interestin'.

Down past the Brown's property you can see what we call Back The Field. It slopes down into a gully, then rises back up. That place where those two hills come together is where the kids from Up The Road swim. We play football on Back The Field, too. This is football without helmets or shoulder pads, where you just line up and bust into each other till your Momma calls you in for supper.

We're coming to another driveway now. The house that's closest to the road is Jack Carvery's. He deals in scrap metal from the dump. Yeah, you've heard about the dump. We'll be comin' to it soon enough; don't hold your breath. Those other houses behind Jack's belong to Carverys, too. Uncle Dook's got a candy store on his first floor. His wife runs it. Then there's Uncle Phum and Aunt Dolly's place.

Who knows where those nicknames come from. Childhood, most likely. Sometimes the nickname becomes the real name. Call somebody what it says

Kids on road walking to Deacon Ralph Jones's house.

on their birth certificate, and they'll look at you like you're crazy.

You're beginnin' to notice that Carvery is a pretty common name around here. So is Brown, Mantley, Howe, and Dixon. You got to be careful who you get involved with — it might be your cousin. Older folks know every root and branch of the family tree, though. They'll keep you out of trouble.

Here's Aunt Hattie Carvery's place. She runs our post office. Address a letter to Africville, Nova Scotia, and it'll get here all right. No, Aunt Hattie. Don't want to see no mail today. Probably nothin' but bills.

Let's go down this other driveway. Bertha Mantley's house is right on The Road. Behind it, there's a small house that gets rented out to different people. And then there's Bully Carvery's place. Don't have to tell you how he got that name. He's a hard rock. You don't want to mess with him.

You say you want to keep going? OK, we'll head back to The Road. Didn't mean to make you nervous. There's Curley Vemb's house. That's his real name, all right. He's a Norwegian. Married an Africville girl and moved out here. Gets along just fine.

Now you're lookin' at a whole string of houses. They

all got front yards to separate 'em. Sarah Byers and Edward Dixon live here. And there's Pooh Izzard's place. Pooh's a prizefighter. Trains up at the Creighton Street Gym. How you doin', Pooh? Good luck in your next fight.

Now we're passin' the homes of Bill Gannon, John Tolliver, and Bub Cassidy. And if you look over to the other side of the road, you'll see the church. Seaview African United Baptist Church, to be exact.

Let's go over to the church, and stop for a minute. Look at the way that white paint gleams in the sun. Look at the steeple standing against the sky. Now, be perfectly quiet. Tune out the sounds of the kids and the cars and the dogs.

Listen close ... can you hear it? Can you hear that sound, coming from the church? It's like a heartbeat ... the heartbeat of Africville. This church is the living, breathing soul of our community. As long as this church is here, *we'll* be here.

We pretty well have to run the church ourselves. Ain't enough money here to pay a full-time minister. We get visitin' preachers from places like the Cornwallis Street Church in the City and Saint Thomas Church in North Preston. Old Reverend Wise used to walk all the way from Lake Loon to preach to us. We've had some of the best in our pulpit — Reverend White, Reverend Skeir, Reverend Oliver and Reverend Coleman.

Now we got Reverend Bryant. On Sundays when he

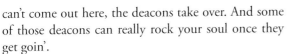

Above and left: Seaview Church was the soul of the community, site of business, Bible classes, meetings and sermons.

We got clubs, youth organizations, ladies' auxiliary, and Bible classes. You want to get somethin' done here, you get it done through the church.

Funny thing — not everybody 'round here goes to church on a regular basis. We got our share of sinners and backsliders: folks who only set foot there on Christmas and Easter, and others who don't set foot there at all and don't mind tellin' you so. But you know what? Even those folks say this is "our" church. It belongs to everybody, whether they go or not.

You ought to come out here next Easter for Sunrise Service. That's the biggest day of the year in Africville. Folks from all over Nova Scotia come here to take part. Got to warn you, though. Be prepared to get up early. Service begins at five in the morning, soon as the sunlight starts fillin' the Basin.

Yes indeed, folks take that day seriously. Most people spend the whole night gettin' their clothes ready and their kids washed. When you're young, you don't even sleep that night. You're wide awake when your Momma comes in to get you up while it's still dark outside.

By the time the preacher's ready to start his sermon, the church is full. You could be listening to Reverend Bryant or maybe somebody from farther away. We sing those old-time spirituals to the tune of organ and

can't come out here, the deacons take over. And some of those deacons can really rock your soul once they get goin'.

And the singin'! You'd have to go a long, long way before you could find singin' like you get here. It's like the people put all their soul in their voices, then send it straight on up to God's ears.

But you know it takes more than singin' and preachin' to make a church. Church got to be more than just a place you get dressed up to go every Sunday. Especially in a place like Africville, where we don't have our own mayor or city council or policemen. Church got to be all those things wrapped up in one. All kinds of business goes on in this church, and not just on Sunday.

Girls attending CGIT.

piano music. If you want to hold hands and sway to the music, that's OK. If you want to stand up and testify, nobody's stoppin' you. Everybody's got their own way to get close to the Lord and each other.

The worship goes on till about noon. Then it's time for the baptism. We do baptisms all year long. But there's something special about being baptized on Easter.

You can see the candidates dressed in their white baptismal robes. They might look a little nervous on the outside, but inside, they're strong. They'll line up behind the Reverend, and then the rest of the congregation lines up behind them. Then the Reverend leads us all from the church down to the Basin. It's a long procession. Each step you take, you realize that your grandparents took it before you, and their grandparents took it before them.

Then we reach the shoreline. Men, women, and children, all lookin' wide-eyed with wonder at the beauty of the Basin. The singin' goes on; it doesn't stop even when the Reverend begins the baptisms. Don't need a choir. The whole congregation is the choir. Our voices

Old school house in Africville, which closed in 1953.

lift up while the candidates get immersed in cold sea-water. Salt water — just like the first baptism that was performed in the Sea of Galilee.

Then we go back to the church. The candidates are wet and happy. Everybody else is happy, too. Some of the people go back to church; others go home to celebrate in their own way. The young ones get to eat all the eggs they want. That's probably what they been thinkin' about all day, anyhow.

Still, some of the meaning of Sunrise Service rubs off on them. One day, they'll be the ones to go into the water. And they'll know this is a day when Africville shines.

Didn't mean to go on like that. But if you want to understand Africville, you got to know about the church. Then again, you heard the heartbeat. So you do understand.

Let's keep goin'. There's more of Africville to see.

Right next to the church is the old school. They closed it down back in '53. We use it for recreation now. See the swings, still standin' in the playground?

It sure was a sad day when that school shut down, and our kids had to walk all the way up to Richmond School from primary on. When children come up from Africville, it's like there's a sign on their forehead saying "Auxiliary Class." You know what that is, don't you? That's where they put the "slow learners."

First thing you got to do at Richmond is prove you're not a "slow learner." Why? Well, once they get you in that Auxiliary Class, you can't get out. It's like bein' caught in a lobster trap. You might as well say your education's over right then and there.

Wasn't like that when we had our own school. Went

Above: Looking out of Dan Dixon's back door.
Left: Gordon Jemmott, teacher for 25 years.
Opposite: Carvery property.

all the way up to Grade 8, it did. Only had one room, but that room was partitioned in two sections. One was for the lower grades, the other for the "big kids." Times bein' what they were, it was hard to stay in school. So many of us had to quit in order to help support our families. But if you could stick it out in that school, you got an education. You could go on to Queen Elizabeth High or Saint Pat's, and know you could hold your own with the other kids.

There was some good teachers at that school. Everybody down here remembers old Mr. Jemmott. Could be even his wife didn't know his first name; he was just "Mister Jemmott." He was from the West Indies. That man taught for twenty-five straight years without missin' a single day. His son, Gordon, ended up bein' the principal. Gordon was just as strict as his old man.

Train going through the centre of the Africville community.

Those black teachers did us proud. John Brown was the first one. Then there were other Jemmotts: Clyde and Clarice. Teachin' sure ran in that family. People remember Laylia Grant and Verna Davis, too. And Portia White taught in our school for a while. Can't that woman sing! But she could teach, too. No doubt about that.

Well, the school's gone now. Can't do nothin' about it. Let's keep goin'.

There's our old friends the triple tracks. Remember

Africville. We'll be goin' there shortly. But there's still more to see right here.

We're gonna be delayed anyhow. Here comes a train. Lord, that noise is terrible. Sounds like an avalanche thunderin' right past you.

There's Dick Killum's house. Look past it, and you'll see a level field. We call it the Southwestern. It's a sports field, mostly. There's some buddies out there now playin' softball. We play horseshoes there, too. In the wintertime, the whole thing freezes over, and you can play hockey on it. You ever hear of the Africville Brown Bombers? The team Gordon Jemmott coached? That's where they practised.

Back in the old days, the Basin used to freeze over, and they played hockey out there. Imagine playin' hockey on part of the Atlantic Ocean! Can't do that nowadays. Winters ain't what they used to be. Nothin' is.

Fellas here play hockey just for the fun of it. Ain't lookin' to get in the NHL. NHL ain't ready for no Jackie Robinson yet, so they say. Every now and then, though, somebody gets ideas. Once there was this boy who wanted to be a goalie. He'd be out there on the Southwestern everyday, stoppin' rubber balls and whatever else kids used instead of pucks.

Well, one day his cousins got hold of a real puck. They started shootin' it around, practisin' the newfangled rifle shot. Buddy figured he was gonna stop that puck just like he stopped all those rubber balls. So he sticks his leg out, with nothin' on it but his pants.

KA-RACKKK!

You could hear the sound all the way over in Big Town. And that's one boy who didn't play no more goal that day.

Train's gone at last. Let's cross the field and go behind that little hill. There's more houses back that way. We're still Up The Road, understand. This is just a different neighbourhood.

Hold it. Got to throw this ball back. Catch it next time, Cousin! Yeah, right! In your dreams!

Those boys wouldn't be so smart if they remembered how good the girls teams were back in the '40s. The Africville Ladies' Softball Club, that's what they called it. White blouses, black skirts and a winnin' attitude. Gordon Jemmott coached them. They used to play all over the province — Stellarton, New Glasgow, places like that. One year, they took the provincial championship.

how they were risin' up? Well, now they're level with us again. We're gonna stop at this bend here. Take a look all around you. Right here is where you can see all of Africville — the whole layout.

Look back where we came from, and you can see Big Town and Up The Road. Now, take a look in the other direction. See those houses peekin' out from behind those woods? That's Round The Bend, the third part of

Kids playing at the pump installed by City at time of relocation.

The three Brown girls were on that team — Lucinda, Jessie, and Ruth. There was Wilhemina and Alma Dixon, Amy Carvery, Stella Dixon, and Evelyn Jemmott, too. Those ladies are all married and settled down now, but you know what? They could still come down here and send those boys runnin' to their Mommas.

There's Aunt Tillie Newman's house. Her daughter Ivory Marsman lives right next door. You can see more houses in a line going toward the water. First there's the old Gannon place. Minky Carvery lives there now. Pauline Dixon and Dora Dixon have the next two houses.

See that shed? That's Uncle John's card room. The men go there when they want to play some serious cards. You don't get cut an inch of slack in *that* shed!

Now we're at a bigger hill. We call this one Uncle Laffy's Hill. That's where kids ride their sleds in the winter. Best time to go down that hill is late at night when the moon's out. Seems like it takes forever before your Momma and Poppa go to sleep. Half the fun is sneakin' out the door with your sled, or piece of cardboard, or whatever you want to use.

When the moon's full or close to it, you might as well be in daylight. It's like the world's turned into one

Young blueberry pickers, Africville.

big black-and-white snapshot. And the kids are part of the picture.

We get up to the top of the hill ... then WHOOOSH! Down we go! When the snow's got a crust of ice on top of it, you zoom down so fast Africville turns into a speeded up movie, everything flashin' past before you can get a good look at it. And you don't make any noise, either. You go zippin' through the trees and between the houses like some kind of ghost.

Well, it sure ain't wintertime now. Tell you who lives up on Uncle Laffy's Hill these days. Whoppie Sparks lives there. He runs a penny store. There's Dixons, Howes and Carverys there, too. And you'll also find Leon and Emma Steed in that neighbourhood. Leon came from the West Indies; Emma is a Carvery.

We could climb up to the top of the hill, but you want to see Round The Bend before it gets dark. So we'll take a different way. We can just skirt around to the other side of the hill and head back to the Southwestern.

You can see the Paris house at the bottom of the hill. Now, look way up. There's the High Track. Remember we crossed it when we first came down Barrington Street? More folks live along the road that follows the track. Another Paris family's up there, and there's more Dixons.

You say you're gettin' thirsty? Let's head to Whoppie's store and get some pop before we go on.

How you doin', Whoppie? Can we get two Cokes? Thanks. Naw, can't stay too long. We're takin' the Grand Tour of Africville. More to it than there seems

Above: Deacon Ralph Jones.
Right: Driving toward the church.
Opposite: Matilda Newman's store.

to be, right? That's what people always say when they come here for the first time. See you later, Whoppie.

Want to show you a couple more houses past the Southwestern before we go Round The Bend. You see the horseshoe curve over there? Roy Mantley lives down that way. So does Lee Carvery. What's that? You say there's more Carverys around here than there are trees? Don't get smart. We can always go back to Uncle Bully's, you know.

Now we're following the curve of the triple tracks. Your nose is wrinklin' already, like it wants to be someplace else. That's a sure sign we're gettin' close to the dump, over on the water side. Doggone thing's only been here a few years, and already people associate it with us. Or us with it. They take our school away and give us a garbage dump!

Above: Around the bend.
Opposite: Dan Dixon and granddaughter.

Well, when bad times hit you, you can just lay down and die. Or you can keep on goin' and make the best of it. So we try to make the dump work for us. Just because somebody throws something away, that don't mean you can't use it.

Looks like a mountain of trash and junk, doesn't it? But it's not all bad. There's all kinds of scrap metal in there that you can collect and sell. Copper, steel, brass, tin — all of it's worth somethin'. You got to know what you're doin', understand. There's ways of tellin' good stuff from bad stuff. You got to learn, just like

any other trade. They call it "salvaging."

Car parts. That's another one. We got fellas here who can get parts off the dump and make the worst lookin' wreck in the world run like new. One time, a couple of buddies put together a whole car from scratch and drove it to Winnipeg. Did they drive it back? Naw. If it didn't fall apart, they probably sold it. Somebody out there now could be drivin' an "Africmobile."

You know what really gets up folks' behinds out here? When those newspapers talk about us "scavenging" food and clothes off the dump. People read that

stuff and think we're runnin' around diggin' week-old tomatoes and nasty rags out of that messy dump. Any fool knows you get stuff off the trucks *before* they throw it on the dump. Doesn't hurt the drivers to give us day-old bread or leftover meat every now and then. They do the same thing for people who live near other dumps.

We get clothes from them, too. By the time the ladies out here get through workin' on second-hand clothes with their needle and thread, you'd never know they were bound for the dump.

Some folks say the dump was put here to try to drive us out. If that's true, things kind of backfired, didn't they?

Well, we could stand here talkin' about this place all day. But it ain't the most pleasant way to spend an afternoon. So let's go Round The Bend.

First houses you see here are Mrs. Thomas's and Dan Dixon's, right off the tracks there. That other house belongs to Lucy Carvery. Up toward the High Track is Deacon George Mantley's place, and right next to it's Willie Carvery's. And then there's Pa Carvery's house. "Uncle Pa," everybody calls him. If he's not your grandfather or great-uncle, he ought to be. Pa's got a little store, too. It's in the other part of Round The Bend, past these woods.

That's right. We got our own little forest here. Used to be a lot more woods and bush around, but most of it got cut down for lumber and firewood. Nothin' but young trees and alder bushes and wildflowers

Above: Lee Carvery and Lil Carvery.
Opposite: Interior of Dan Dixon's house.

now. We'll just follow this little path here, and we'll be all right.

See that pond over there? We call it our "lake," even though it ain't really all that big. When the sun hits it right, it looks just like a jewel.

No need to be scared of that dog. Any dog that shouldn't be loose, we keep chained in a shed. Don't tell that to the cops, though. Some of 'em come up here with their huntin' jackets on and shoot our dogs like they was in season.

Go on home, boy. That's right. Got nothin' for you here.

Well, that's the end of the woods. We're in the last part of Africville. Some of those houses we're lookin' at now got runnin' water and indoor toilets. They're far away from all that "unbreakable" rock the City keeps tellin' us about when we want to get water lines put in.

There's Lully Byers's house. Yeah, that's Lully hangin' her wash on the line. Her real name's Wilhemina. But don't ever call her that, or she'll hang *you* out to dry!

There's Rossie Dixon's. And the Emersons's. Reggie and Stella Carvery are here, and Ronald and Sooks Howe. Pa Carvery's store's out here, too.

Did you know Joe Louis stayed at Rossie's house one night? Yeah, Joe Louis. The Brown Bomber himself. We used to listen to his fights all the time on Jamesie Paris's radio. He had one of those old RCA radios with the big horn.

You remember when Joe came to Halifax a few years ago to referee some rasslin' matches? That's how he had to make his livin' when he gave up the heavyweight title and then couldn't get it back.

Anyhow, the promoter for the rasslin' put him up in one of those downtown hotels that usually don't take coloured guests. Well, when Joe got wind of that, he checked right out of that hotel. You know how Joe

Above: Duke Ellington, American composer, pianist and big band leader, visited Africville.
Opposite: Oulton girls in backyard.

was. Never would put up with no discrimination.

Then off Joe went lookin' for the coloured folks' part of town, and he ended up here. When he found out he'd been stayin' with a Dixon, he just lit right up with a smile. Turns out he knew all about George Dixon, the first coloured man to win any kind of prizefightin' championship. Well, you know George was born in Africville, and every Dixon here is some kind of relation of his. So Joe felt right at home, stayin' with a Dixon.

Seemed like half of Halifax was out here lookin' to shake Joe's hand or get his autograph. That was some night for Africville, let me tell you. When Joe left the next day, he looked like he was sorry he had to go.

But you know, Joe Louis wasn't the only famous person to come to Africville. Remember Reggie and Stella Carvery's place? Well, Duke Ellington stops by there all the time. That's right, the one and only Duke. There's a story behind that, too.

Duke's wife's name is Mildred Dixon. She was born in Boston, but her father was an Africville Dixon, and he never forgot where he came from. Stella Carvery's a Dixon, too — Mildred's her cousin.

Mildred was a ballet dancer. Duke took one look at her and BOOM — he was in love. They got married down in New York.

Now Mildred was Duke's second wife. He had a son named Mercer by his first one. Mildred was the one who raised Mercer; far as he was concerned, she was his Momma. And every time Duke brings his band to Halifax, he comes out here to see his in-laws. Mercer comes this way, too. And Duke gives us free tickets to his concerts.

Remember that song of his, "Sophisticated Lady"? That's about Mildred. Next time you listen to the Duke's music, maybe you'll remember there's a little bit of Africville in it.

You know, that's one of the reasons why we don't pay much mind when people talk down to us. If we're good enough for folks like Joe Louis and Duke Ellington, we figure we're darn well good enough for anybody else.

Well, we're just about at the end of our trip. The

Highways Board Building and the Fairview Overpass — that's the end of Africville.

Sure, you're welcome to stick around. Stop by for supper, we'll be glad to have you. Stay over night too, if you want. Always room for one more here.

And when you get back home, if anybody asks you about Africville, you just tell 'em we been through good times and hard times, but we're still here. Yeah, there's been talk about gettin' us out of here. "Relocation" they call it. But we've heard that kind of talk before. Long as it's just talk, we got nothin' to worry about, right?[1]

CHAPTER 2
AFRICVILLE: AN HISTORICAL OVERVIEW

DONALD CLAIRMONT

Until the heavy immigration of West Indians in recent decades, Nova Scotia was considered to have been the major centre of the black experience in Canada. Of all the Nova Scotian black communities, Africville has undoubtedly been the best known. Books, national and international magazine articles, television and radio programs, poetry and song — all have told the story of this small black community which was bulldozed out of existence in the late 1960s, but which spiritually and symbolically has resisted burial.

Africville was an exceptional community and a symbol for the struggle against racism and segregation in Nova Scotia. While it was viewed negatively by Whites and Blacks alike, the community was nevertheless a magnet for both groupings. In addition, Africville represented the essence of the black experience in Nova Scotia — in its church soul, in its struggle against racism and even in its location, off the beaten path, on the fringe of the white neighbourhoods. Although it was seen as a haven for the dispossessed, it was a community where most of the residents could trace their kinship ties to the founding families, over a hundred years earlier.

SETTLEMENT AND EARLY YEARS
The origins of the people of Africville and the settlement of Africville are uncertain. The first documented transaction was a purchase of land in January 1848 by William Brown and William Arnold.

While it was within the city's boundaries, nevertheless, Africville was separated from the mainstream of

Children playing by old school foundation, 1963.

the City, firstly by being a black community in a racist society, secondly by its location. Whether the yardstick was the provision of City services, positive concern by City officials, historical accounts by black and white writers, or even many residents' own perception, Africville was always on its own.

The strong community spirit of Africville and the enduring desire for educational opportunities recur several times in the community's history. After much unsuccessful petitioning of government and years of informal teaching provided by a resident, an elementary school was established in 1883. At that time, communities were responsible for funding their own schools and racism often excluded "coloured children" from the common schools. The school served Africville

until 1953 at which time it was closed and the children transferred to integrated schools elsewhere in Halifax.

Throughout its first half-century, Africville was quite rural in character. Goats, chickens and horses were commonplace, and fishing in the Bedford Basin was as much a part of the way of life as paid employment. The land was not suitable for farming but several people kept pigs, as well as growing vegetables. The population remained small as many Africville residents, like other Nova Scotians, migrated to the more prosperous "Boston States" in the last third of the nineteenth century.

In those early days, life in Africville was hard. Economically the first and second generation residents were not prosperous. Jobs were scarce and racism helped channel Blacks into low-paying employment.

Africville neighbourhood, c. 1958 (school foundation in foreground).

Few residents attained more than a rudimentary education in their school.

Nevertheless, the difference between Africville and other communities, including other areas of the City of Halifax, was not overwhelming. Africville was always a viable community with some fine houses, plenty of space, some small-scale entrepreneurs and a strong community spirit.

THE GOOD YEARS

It was lovely, lovely. They talk about Peggy's Cove but I am going to tell you, it was the most beautiful sight you could want to see — Africville. You could get on a hill and look over Bedford Basin in the fall of the year, say from October to around December, and there was a sight to see, especially at twilight when the sun is sinking over the hills at Bedford ... And another thing, during the war ... when the convoys were in the Basin, there was another beautiful sight. It was one of the most beautiful spots I've been in, in Nova Scotia. (Leon Steed, Africville resident)

Interviewed in the 1960s, virtually all the very elderly Africvilleans reminisced happily about their early years. They related stories of their parents riding on horseback through the woods around Africville; they talked of skating on the Bedford Basin and of riding the trains into the North Street Station. Others, referring to these early years as good years, recalled the greater independence of the residents and the greater well-being of the community in contrast to their experience in the later period.

Africville census report, year unknown.

Evidence from census data indicates that Africvilleans performed a wide variety of work between the early settlement days and the First World War. Most Africville men were employed over the years in general labour and low-paid service work. In addition to truckmen who hauled away household waste, there were stonemasons and barrel-makers, longtime occupational specializations of Blacks in Halifax County.

Most of the people who reported themselves as seamen had worked the ships travelling between Halifax and the West Indies, and they had subsequently settled down in Africville. Within the immediate area some short-term stevedoring work, especially loading or unloading coal, was available, as was heavy, dirty work toting bags of fertilizer in a nearby bone-meal plant.

Africville women worked what is now often called the "double day." A number were employed sewing bags in the bone-meal plant but most were employed as servants and washerwomen. Some of the elderly Africville women cleaned houses in Richmond, the north end of Halifax, following the tradition of their own mothers. Government institutions hired Africville women to cook and clean and several were employed in the hospital and the prison overlooking the community.

THE AFRICVILLE CHURCH

A church congregation was formally established in 1849. When it joined with other black Baptist congregations to form the African Baptist Association in 1854 at Granville Mountain, its pastor was the association's founder, the great Richard Preston. Preston was also pastor of several other congregations at that time.

Although Africville never had a resident pastor, the church was always the fundamental institution in the community, and the deacons who directed the church represented Africville to outside authorities.

Social life in the first fifty years revolved around the church, with special activities that brought together both the church-going and the other members of the community. Baptisms, weddings and funerals held in

Above: 2nd Battalion WWI marching band. Men at this time were employed in a variety of labour and service work. Right: Mrs. Elsie Desmond. Women of Africville often worked a "double day."

the church fostered a sense of community. Especially significant in this regard was the Sunrise Service on Easter Sunday, a colourful occasion like other community festivities for which Africville was well known; one resident described the service as follows:

> *They [church members led by the deacons] went into the church singing spirituals, around four or five o'clock in the morning when the sun came up, and did not come out till three p.m.... People, including Whites, used to come from miles around to the sunrise service, sometimes from Truro and New Glasgow and usually from Preston and Hammonds Plains.*

Above: Events such as weddings at the church fostered a sense of community.
Left: Millie and Benny Jones.

Also, through the church Africvilleans were linked to the other black communities in Halifax County and to white congregations in the City. Africville was frequently the site selected for the picnic activities of other black church organizations, and throughout the years, numerous members of the African Baptist Association were baptised by being led into the waters at Africville. In 1874, the Reverend J. Thomas conducted one of the largest baptisms on record in the Halifax area, with forty-six candidates; the ceremony, it was reported, "attracted a large concourse of persons from the City."

THE NAME "AFRICVILLE"

In its early years the community was named after the

Africville was populated almost entirely by black families from a wide variety of origins.

road around which it grew, namely Campbell Road. "Africville" became current around the turn of the century, though this name does appear as early as the 1860s in several petitions to government and in some land deeds. In the nineteenth century both "African" and "Men of Colour" were common descriptive terms. "African village" was perhaps the equivalent of the contemporary expression "black community." Railroad documents around 1860 referring to business dealings in the area used the phrase "African Village;" the first reference to the settlement as Africville in the minutes of Halifax City Council was in 1867.

When the Baptist church was established in the community it was designated the Campbell Road congregation. In 1885 its name was changed to Africville but in 1893 church members requested of the African Baptist Association a reversion to the original name. It was later changed to the Seaview African United Baptist Church. Nevertheless, by the twentieth century the name "Africville" was firmly in place. In the years ahead, mail was sent to persons in "Africville;" the local, segregated school bore the name, as did local athletic teams and other voluntary associations.

Interviewed at the time of relocation, Africvilleans had mixed feelings about the name. There was a consensus that it had been imposed by white Haligonians "because our ancestors came from Africa." At the same time there was ambivalence towards the name since it

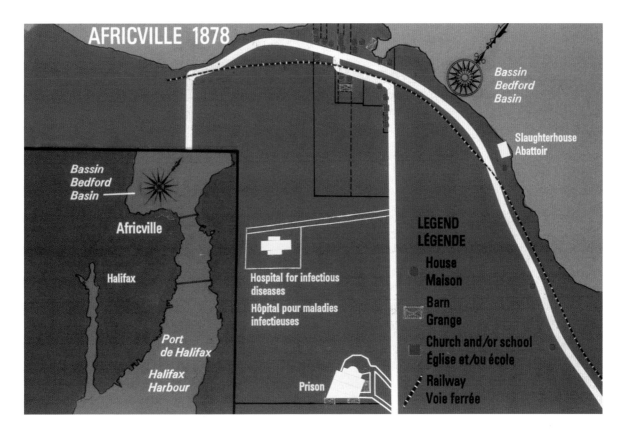

AFRICVILLE 1878

Bassin
Bedford
Basin

Slaughterhouse
Abattoir

Bassin
Bedford
Basin

Africville

Halifax

Port
de Halifax

Halifax
Harbour

Hospital for infectious
diseases
Hôpital pour maladies
infectieuses

Prison

**LEGEND
LÉGENDE**

House
Maison

Barn
Grange

Church and/or school
Église et/ou école

Railway
Voie ferrée

Above: Map of Africville showing buildings near settlement.
Right: The city dump, a health menace, was moved close to Africville homes.

highlighted racial differences in a racist society. One elderly resident, very conscious of her people's ancestry in American slavery, was scornful of the African designation: "It wasn't Africville out there. None of the people came from Africa. You better believe it. It was part of Richmond [northern Halifax], just the part where the coloured folks lived." Some other elderly residents were more favourably disposed to the appellation, Africville, and hostile to "meddlers" who would have it otherwise.

THE DEVELOPING COMMUNITY

As Africville was developing so too was the rest of the City, and the idyllic rural setting was eventually shattered by the roaring of trains and the buzzing of industries. The population of Halifax more than doubled between 1851 and 1915, and the City permitted industrial growth along the shores of the peninsula to encroach on the residential area of Africville. Just a few hundred metres from the settlement a bone-meal plant manufacturing fertilizer was

City dump on fire.

constructed. A cotton factory, rolling mill/nail factory, slaughterhouse and port facility for handling coal completed the first ring of encirclement; beyond this were other factories and foundries.

Railroad tracks were laid straight through the community in the 1850s, and subsequently expanded twice before the First World War. Land was expropriated from Africville residents for this purpose and they learned to live with the railway in their midst. The Halifax Civic Planning Commission recognized that these developments produced "blight and decay spreading over large areas, thereby resulting in serious reduction of residential values," yet they took no steps to prevent this deterioration of the community.

Moreover, racism and the residents' lack of economic or political influence made the area a choice site for City service facilities not wanted elsewhere. Under citizens'

pressure, the City closed sewage disposal pits in the southend of Halifax and relocated them on the edge of Africville in 1858. They had the Infectious Diseases Hospital built on the hill overlooking the community in the 1870s, followed by the Trachoma Hospital in 1903. Such developments continued into the twentieth century with, for example, a stone-crushing plant and an abattoir on the edges of the settlement. Finally, the culmination was reached in the mid-1950s when the City moved the large open City dump, labelled a health menace by City Council and resisted by residents in other areas, to a site just 100 metres from the westernmost group of Africville homes.

Halifax City Council minutes clearly indicate that in addition to using this area for facilities not tolerated in other neighbourhoods, the eventual industrial use of Africville lands was planned. As Halifax was

Above: Brown Bombers hockey team, with many Africville members.
Right: Gerald Johnson, his brother Charles and his nephew Robert.

experiencing industrial expansion, there were several resolutions adopted by Council to expropriate the Africville lands. While for one reason or another these resolutions were not acted upon, the City's policy was spelled out in the following, a response to an interested business in 1915:

> *The Africville portion of Campbell Road will always be an industrial district and it is desirable that industrial operations should be assisted in any way that is not prejudiced to the interests of the public; in fact, we may be obliged in the future to consider the interests of industry first.*

Above: Reception at Community Hall to celebrate the return of Africville's WWII veterans, 1945. Front L to R: Leo Carvery, Wilburt Kelly, Ross Dixon, Reginald Carvery, Stanley Dixon, Leonard Dixon, Moses Grant, Willard Clayton, Lester Carvery, David Dixon. Back L to R: Walter Johnston, Mr. Ferguson, Mrs. Florence David, Deacon Ralph Jones, Reverend William P. Oliver, Mrs. Hattie Carvery, Deacon Fred Carvery, Mrs. Amy Dixon, Gordon Jemmott, Mrs. Stella Carvery, Mrs. Elsie Desmond.
Opposite: There were a few horses and barns in the settlement, since several men carted materials.

In 1916, at the request of Africville residents, City Council agreed to the use of City-owned property as the site for a new church in the community. A short-term lease was granted with the City engineer's recommendation as follows:

It is not desirable that the City should part with any of its property in Africville for any such purpose, as it is probable that in the near future, all property in this district will be required for industrial purposes and it will be abandoned as a residential district.

Throughout this early period as Africville's residential value was diminishing, there was little evidence in official records of any concern about the devaluation of properties, nor about what might happen to Africville residents had the land they occupied been expropriated, nor, indeed, what their wishes may have been. In fact, there is no record of any concern for the health and safety of the Africville residents in relation to the hazards posed by these developments. One Africville resident summed up the situation saying, "They said the people in Africville encroached on the government but I would say the government encroached on the people."

Apart from a limited amount of employment, Africville residents gained little direct benefit from any of the adjacent developments. And as the City had designated the area for industrial use, residential building plans by Africvilleans received only short shrift from the City.

The lives of Africville residents, in fact, were negatively affected by industrial development and by the City's unwillingness to provide services. Complaints and petitions, whether for police services, building permits, or garbage pickup, fell on deaf ears, and over time the community came to expect only disinterest and disregard for their requests by the City.

This was clearly illustrated in the City's treatment of an important Africville petition in 1919. Partly as a consequence of developments relating to the First World War and partly as a natural unfolding of the City's negative attitudes and practices, bootlegging and

Bible school class.

raucous living had became a serious problem for the community. Many residents collaborated in preparing the following petition to City Council in June 1919:

We, the undersigned ratepayers, do hereby make application for better police protection at Africville. We base our application on the following grounds: that a police officer seldom or never visits this district, except for a warrant or subpoena; the conditions that now prevail here are worse that at any time before; that these lamentable conditions tend to turn the majority away from the good teaching which they have received; that there is now an utter disregard of the Lord's Day by many residents; that there are many persons, strangers in our midst, living openly in a state of debauchery, which must corrupt the minds of youth, for we are more or less subject to our environment; that there is nightly confusion, carousel and dissipation which disturb the peaceful night; that

these carousels have been the centres for spreading infection throughout the village; that we believe, if this disgraceful state of affairs continues there will be grave crime or crimes committed. Our earnest desire is that your Honourable Body, in this period of reconstruction, carefully consider our application so that the omission of the past may be rectified and by your assistance the evil influence now at work may be greatly reduced; then shall we be better able to train the young in the way of good citizenship and place the village on a better plane of Social Welfare.

Like other Africville petitions and protests, this one was dismissed by City officials. While other Haligonians enjoyed police protection, the petitioners were advised that "the City department had no spare men to send such a distance," that the residents should "form their own police department and anyone they appoint to act as a policeman, the Mayor would swear

Early '60s, Seaview African United Baptist Church.

in as a Special Constable" and that "in the event of any serious trouble being reported, the Chief is always in a position to send a squad to this district."

Reconstructing the history of Africville through records and interviews, one could almost sense the drop in community spirit and morale that followed upon this blatant acknowledgement of their powerlessness in obtaining comparable services with other parts of the City.

A COMMUNITY, ISOLATED AND VULNERABLE

Subsequent to World War One, Africville became increasingly vulnerable to relocation plans. Most residents continued to press for changes and coped as best they could. Frustrated, some ambitious and regularly-employed residents moved out of the community to obtain modern services and other opportunities, or they encouraged their children to do so. Disadvantaged

and problem-laden persons, black and white, some displaced by developments in the City centre, moved in, usually as renters on Africville land and sometimes occupying City property. The growth of population and the informality of property boundaries combined with this modest influx of renters, created an image of disorganization. The influence of church leaders also began to wane as it was clear that they could not bring about any progressive action by the City. Africville's social problems grew and it acquired a bad reputation among both Blacks and Whites in the Halifax area.

Several Blacks from other parts of Halifax and beyond recalled, in interviews, that they were warned by their parents against ever going to Africville. Increasingly, Africville became stereotyped as a slum, a hazardous place, a community of "drifters." This exaggeration weighed heavily on the many sixth-generation residents who bore keen memories of past struggles and past glories, and it belied what one writer has aptly

Africville neighbourhood (the white house with the sun porch was the post office), c. 1958.

called the true story of the community, namely "the story of many persons who have managed to keep their pride despite circumstances that would have ground many of us under." For example, Africville produced a world champion boxer, George Dixon, and an ordained minister, Edward Dixon; and a nationally recognized singer, Portia White, taught in its school. In addition, of course, this view disregarded the many well-kept homes and the community-spirited people striving to keep the flame alive, no matter what the odds.

Throughout this period, from the end of the First World War to the time of relocation, the City's attitude towards Africville did not change. The emphasis was on eliminating the community rather than helping it. One elderly relocatee noted in 1968: "Ever since I was old enough to understand, they [City officials] were talking about relocation. They talked about it so much that we thought it would never happen."

The gap between services and facilities available in Africville and those provided elsewhere in the City widened. While the rest of Halifax evolved into an attractive, modern urban site, the City failed to pave the roads in Africville. The City did not provide garbage and snowplow service, water and sewerage facilities, or building-code enforcement. Officials justified this by saying that the City had zoned the area for industrial development. Failure to make improvements and to

provide services went on even in the face of known health hazards. For example, the makeshift wells in Africville ran dry in the summer and were a constant threat to health. In 1954 the City Manager noted:

The water supply in Africville is from shallow wells which show more contamination than is desirable. The proximity of privies to these wells is particularly bad with the rocky soil conditions. The City of Halifax has been fortunate that no serious health conditions have resulted from this situation.

In the aftermath of a major fire in 1947, the future of Africville was publicly debated. City staff and aldermen for the most part reiterated the view that rather than extending water and sewerage to Africville, "the property ... be cleared in case some industry might want to go there." For once, Africville residents were consulted on the matter. They expressed a strong desire to remain in the area and to work with the City in developing the community. Their views were ignored.

In 1957 a fire in Africville claimed the lives of three children. The absence of a water main and hydrants in Africville made the community very vulnerable and also prevented residents from obtaining insurance coverage. In the early 1960s, after a fire had destroyed one of the best homes in the community, the deputy fire chief said "the location is inaccessible and the lack of hydrants added to our difficulty." The victim, whose home was not insured, was quoted as saying:

We have all tried up here to get a proper water supply. Two houses have burned in the last five years. But it's hopeless; they just won't do anything for us.

A strong sense of alienation and powerlessness was left in the community. Clearly, the City was unwilling to provide services. Yet protests and petitions continued and sometimes there were small victories. In the late 1930s, for example, Africville residents successfully petitioned for their own postal suboffice (prior to this they had to walk ten kilometres to mail letters), for a few street lights and for street numbers. The sense that the community would never be properly developed as a fully serviced urban site caused potential leaders to migrate, especially in the period immediately following the Second World War. One local black authority on Africville observed:

There seemed to be in the community the feeling that nothing could happen anyway, sort of pessimistic, not cynical, but a lack of confidence and a feeling that nothing is going to happen and if it does, so what? There is nothing we can do about it. They tried in so many ways to get little improvements. They tried for ordinary services ... and they failed.... You see, the community had reached a stage where it became a sort of haven, a refuge for the people who couldn't keep their heads above the water in the City, [sic] not the stable and solid families that settled the community initially. This brought out a change in the community and in the community spirit.

As might be expected, there were corresponding changes in the vitality of the church. Baptisms became

The Rangers baseball team with many Africville members.

less frequent and by 1960 only a handful of the baptized residents were under forty years of age. Regular church attendance declined, rarely exceeding thirty. In the years just before relocation, the church was rarely opened except for services, limited to one each Sunday. A minister who served Africville during the 1950s observed that "the church was the only organization [the Africville residents] had and then, the church only had a few people who were interested."

The church elders became less influential as both they and others acknowledged powerlessness; as one deacon observed in 1968: "The government is a powerful machine to fight against. They will use their power to defeat you. That is why I was one of the first families to move from Africville [at the time of relocation]."

THE STRUGGLE FOR COMMUNITY

Despite the racism, the stigmatization, the City neglect, the loss of much leadership potential through out-migration and the decline of the church's day-to-day leadership, Africville continued to be a viable and valued community. It was still a place where everyone knew one another, and where most people were related by kinship to one another and to the original settlers. As noted, when consulted by City officials in 1948, the residents indicated their desire to stay and develop the community with some government assistance. And in the 1950s, when for a while building permits were being issued, fifteen residents (of the sixteen who applied) obtained permits to repair their dwellings or erect new structures.

The church continued to have profound symbolic importance for Africvilleans. It was the soul, the historical continuity, of the community, the tangible evidence of value, but it was not an effective vehicle for practical social change. Perhaps the Africvilleans' profound struggle was reflected in the often moving church services for which the Africville congregation

Men along railroad tracks, Africville.

was well known. One local black minister who served several churches in the area commented in an interview in 1968:

> *If you know anything about soul music today ... they had it in Africville. I always made a point when I really wanted to put some life in my church, I brought them in. Whenever I announced that the Africville group would be there, the church would be filled.*

Like any genuine community, Africville was always being rejuvenated by new generations and new leaders even as it was being battered by formidable forces. Compromises had to be made, but the struggle for community and well-being was always there, and perhaps the successes were especially meaningful given the adversities.

ON THE EVE OF RELOCATION

In 1959 the Institute of Public Affairs, at Dalhousie University, conducted a survey of socio-economic conditions among Blacks in Halifax. Data from this survey provide a snapshot of Africville just prior to relocation.

- 50 per cent of the 394 residents were under 15 years old (compared to 25 per cent in all Halifax)
- 35 per cent of the labour force had regular employment
- 70 per cent of employed persons worked as domestics/cleaners or labourers/stevedores
- 20 per cent of the 80 households had earned income of more than $3,000 (compared to over 80 per cent in all Halifax)
- 50 per cent of the labour force had earned income of less than $1,000 (compared to less than 5 per cent in all Halifax)
- 40 per cent of adults had reached Grade 6 or less

Burning dump.

(five persons had reached Grade 10)
- 60 per cent of children were behind in educational achievement (only one child was beyond Grade 7)

The survey asked household heads about their views on living in the community. Roughly sixty-five per cent of the respondents reported their liking for living in Africville and their reluctance to move. About one quarter both disliked living there and said that they would be willing movers. Most of these were household heads who had married into the community and who were most likely to be regularly employed and earn over $3,000 annually. These people were also among the most vocal members in the community.

However disadvantaged Africville residents may have been in terms of jobs, income, education and amenities, the community provided much of value for its members. For a wide variety of reasons most residents wanted to stay there and develop the community. Africville residents often used mid-city Blacks as their reference on housing and general lifestyle, and they noted that Africville "was better than in the City, better than some of those slums downtown." They added that the cost of accommodation was also substantially less in Africville.

While the church was still the only community organization, Africville residents enjoyed a rich, informal and neighbourly life. And despite the poor conditions, most adults expressed optimism that their children would have a better life without needing to relocate. According to the 1959 survey, the number one concern of household heads was not housing or

In the late '50s households in Africville were primarily concerned with their children's education.

jobs but the quality of education that the children were receiving.

In sum, on all the socio-economic indicators noted above, namely size of dependent population, work, income and education, the Africville averages were less favourable than those of Blacks and Whites elsewhere in the City. And of course the lack of City services, the difficulty of securing any kind of fire insurance and City Hall's indifference to zoning, building and other specifications meant that housing varied in quality and land ownership was often not clear. Personal pride and community tradition accounted for the fact that so many homes were presentable, especially on the inside. The best housing was in the main settlement area where all the homes had electricity and about fifteen had stone or cement foundations. Still, only nineteen

properties were assessed at more than $1,000 in 1962, and but a handful were assessed for more than $3,000 (compared to 95 per cent of Halifax homes).

In 1964 Reverend W.P. Oliver, the distinguished black leader in Nova Scotia and former pastor to Africville, writing as regional representative of the Adult Education Division of the Nova Scotia Department of Education, noted the substandard level of City services to the area: "The community presents a picture of neglect, poor roads, primitive and unsanitary wells and outside privies."

City officials tried to blame residents rather than accept responsibility for the substandard services. They said that the costs of existing City services (educational and welfare services) to Africville far exceeded the taxes levied and that much tax was in arrears. They were also

quick to cite appraisal reports which contended in 1961 that "only thirteen deeds could be documented" and "there were no more than two lots as marketable commodity [sic] with legal title in Africville." The City implied that Africville was getting "a good deal" and that they could not expect more than they were receiving. The failure of the City to see its own role in Africville's lower standards is another illustration of racism towards the community.

By the 1950s, the decade before relocation, the vast majority of Africville residents were black and deeply rooted in the community, having lived there all their lives. When the relocation push came from City officials in the early 1960s, the residents were economically hard-pressed and poorly organized. The social structure of the community was complex. Sixth-generation residents rubbed shoulders with white transients. A strong church tradition co-existed with a widespread and largely false reputation of raucous living.

Essentially, Africville was a community with an exceptional sense of historical continuity, but its residents lacked political power and influence with City officials. In addition, outsiders, black and white alike, could not see Africville as viable and its existence as desirable. To appreciate its spirit, one had to know the community from the inside — its history, its struggles, and above all, the value of the community to its residents.[2]

CHAPTER 3

MOVING PEOPLE:
RELOCATION AND URBAN RENEWAL

DONALD CLAIRMONT

In the 1950s and 1960s, urban renewal and public housing construction became commonplace in cities throughout Canada and the United States. In Canada, under the partnership funding of federal, provincial and municipal governments, programs were designed to demolish and rebuild downtown areas. The people displaced by these plans were usually of low socio-economic status, often racial and ethnic minorities. Their homes, sometimes labelled "slums," were destroyed and the area developed for business or institutional purposes. The displaced persons were often offered rent-subsidized public housing, owned and managed by a municipal housing commission.

The people promoting urban renewal emphasized economic revitalization, beautification, the elimination of slums and the provision of more adequate housing for the disadvantaged. Such programs were part of a widespread pattern of relocation and social development carried out by government during this period. Large relocations took place in Newfoundland, in the Canadian North and elsewhere.

In urban renewal the demolition of housing in one area and the relocation of its residents was justified on the grounds that both the city and the residents would benefit. Beautification and civic pride, attracting industry and increased revenue from taxes were among the expected civic benefits. The residents who were directly affected would presumably receive better housing — usually public housing.

Nevertheless, the formulation and implementation of urban renewal was controlled by politicians and planners, usually in close collaboration with developers. They assumed that the outcome would benefit the relocated residents even when the people affected disagreed and said so.

In the situations where the residents' needs were considered, the

Well across from Bertha Mantley's house.

assumption was that lifestyle and life opportunities of the disadvantaged could be improved by being displaced and moved to new, presumably higher-quality housing. By combining programs of educational upgrading, job-skills training and counselling with dramatic change in housing, urban renewal could solve poverty and other social problems.

Extensive American research indicated that the most obvious beneficiaries of urban renewal were the developers, the business interests and citizens best situated to profit from economic growth, e.g. construction workers, professionals etc. The relocated persons were frequently moved into other substandard housing complexes, and hopes of new life opportunities proved illusory. It was no wonder that critics saw urban

renewal as a race and class struggle.

In Canada, major pioneering urban renewal projects in Toronto in the mid-1950s and early 1960s received positive evaluations by the original planners. The large public housing areas that were constructed for relocatees (e.g. Toronto's Regent Park, Alexandra Park) were deemed by researchers to represent improved housing. Studies indicated that people relocated in public housing fared better and were more satisfied than those who moved into private housing, though this comparison said more about the substandard condition of the private housing people moved into than it did about the quality of public housing.

Large rent-subsidized public housing complexes did provide better housing than people could afford

City Council suggesting wholesale relocation might be imminent. Two events in particular translated this long-standing intent into reality, namely the Stephenson Report of 1957 and the creation of the City's Department of Development in 1961. These events, in turn, relate back to the modernization and growth of Halifax and the launching of widespread urban renewal in Canada.

Stimulated by the Second World War, Halifax — and Canada generally — experienced significant population and economic growth in the decade, 1945–55. By 1956, its population had reached 93,000, a four-fold increase since 1856 and within the same City boundaries. The surrounding metropolitan area was also growing rapidly, gaining an additional 60,000 people between the end of the war and 1956. Industrial development, especially on the waterfront, was steadily advancing, and the peninsula of Halifax was clearly being "pushed to its limits." Also, as in other Canadian cities at this time, Council was setting up committees to examine housing problems and relate to new urban renewal programs launched by the two senior levels of government.

The Halifax branch of the Community Planning Association of Canada, an influential voluntary organization of planners, politicians and high status community activists, pressed for housing reform and modernization. They encouraged the City to hire a noted city planner, Gordon Stephenson, Professor of Town and Regional Planning, University of Toronto, to investigate housing conditions and needs and to recommend redevelopment policies for Halifax.

Stephenson recommended urban renewal and redevelopment schemes for several areas of Halifax, including Africville. In his report he commented on Africville as follows:

There is a little frequented part of the City, overlooking Bedford Basin, which presents an unusual problem for any community to face. In what may be described as an encampment, or shack town, there live some seventy negro families....

The citizens of Africville live a life apart. On a sunny day, the small children roam at will in a spacious area and swim in what amounts to their private lagoon. In winter, life is far from idyllic. In terms of the physical condition of buildings and sanitation, the story is deplorable. Shallow wells and cesspools, in close proximity, are scattered about the

on the private market.

Apart from housing standards, urban renewal in Canada received positive assessments since, unlike much American experience, it did not appear to destroy social networks and generate profound social uprooting. For example, persons displaced by urban renewal in Toronto and in Winnipeg tended to maintain their social networks and in any event, they had an average length of residence in their area of less than ten years.

HALIFAX AND THE "AFRICVILLE PROBLEM"

As noted in Chapter 2, the relocation of Africville people and the use of the land for industrial or services purposes had been favoured by the City for many decades. Indeed, several minor relocations had occurred over the years to accommodate railway expansion and many policy statements had been advanced in

Above: A home being inspected for demolition.
Left: Participant at a public meeting held at Seaview Church.

slopes between the shacks.

There are only two things to be said. The families will have to be rehoused in the near future. The land which they now occupy will be required for the future development of the City.

The report conveyed a tone and outlook on Africville that was commonplace among the experts, professionals and even activists who became involved in determining the community's future. It avoided the question of the City's responsibility in the state of the community. Africville was identified more as a problem than an opportunity, and its people were objects of pity, not justice. Rightly indignant about external conditions in the community, the outsiders had little knowledge of the history of community and its past struggles, and they

While politicians may have scorned townspeople's lack of opposition to relocation, the decision seemed to have been already made.

put very little value on the idea of community.

In identifying the value of the land for industrial and harbour development, the Stephenson Report echoed the City's past deliberations and stimulated further activity by City staff in planning for expropriation, plans that were already afoot. In 1954 a report was approved by Council to expropriate the Africville property for industrial purposes and solve "the long-standing problem of Africville" by moving the community en masse to a properly serviced and laid-out site on City-owned property about 3 kilometres away; the report was never acted upon. In 1957 the City did expropriate some property owned by an Africville resident for a proposed Industrial Mile, a land assembly on the basin shore. While this project failed to materialize, the concept was incorporated in the City's 1962 North Shore Development Plan which

called for "a limited access expressway to pass through the Africville district which is slated for removal starting in the spring;" this plan, too, was never implemented as such.

Although little concrete action took place with respect to these redevelopment proposals, the heightened activity and the great number of reports and council motions were clear signals of the City's eagerness to use the land for industrial growth. At the same time, momentum was building on the housing front too, as a result of the Stephenson Report. In 1961, Council's Housing Policy Review Committee recommended clearance of existing housing in Africville.

With the establishment of a Development Department in the same year to coordinate all phases of the development and redevelopment of the City, including an urban renewal program, the die was cast — "to

Participants at a public meeting at Seaview Church.

examine and recommend a solution to the Africville problem" was now a key priority for the department. City staff reports were prepared arguing that, although Africvilleans were reluctant to relocate, complete relocation on an individual household basis was the only realistic way.

Large-scale programs had been implemented in the north and central areas of the City, close to Africville. A large public housing complex, Mulgrave Park, had been built to house the many low-income black and white families relocated by these developments and more public housing was being planned. In terms of either the number of people or the number of homes affected by the overall urban renewal at this time, Africville was to account for less than 10 per cent of the City's relocation up to 1965.

The City's approach was to place priority on urban economics and beautification, not the needs of the uprooted residents.

In the Development Department report in July 1962

the elimination of Africville was recommended. The cost of acquisition and clearance of Africville property was estimated at between $40,000 and $70,000. Africville residents would be offered alternative housing in unsegregated, subsidized rental public housing. Residents without legal title to the land where their house stood would receive a payment of $500 as compensation for yielding their homes to the City. Residents with proof of land ownership — and it was felt this would be a small number — could claim compensation through the courts or in negotiation with the City.

There was nothing in this plan about the historical injustices, nothing about the community life and nothing about new life opportunities for the people. In October 1962, Halifax City Council adopted this relocation proposal unanimously.

AFRICVILLE'S RESPONSE

The day after the report of the Development Department was released to the press, J. Ahern, the

MLA for the area, called for a public meeting in Africville. He argued that relocation was unnecessary and certainly unwanted by Africvilleans, adding "Africville could be developed into one of the finest residential districts in Halifax at a very low cost."

One evening in August 1962, local politicians and some one hundred Africville residents and supporters crowded into the small Seaview African United Baptist Church. As in 1948 when the City asked for residents' views, and as in 1959 when the Institute of Public Affairs undertook its survey, the Africvilleans strongly rejected relocation and urged that they be allowed to stay in Africville and develop it according to City specifications.

No momentum of community protest or political leadership developed from this public meeting. Rather, any potential for protest or continued resistance was redirected by the City staff and well-intentioned outsiders. Africville's response to imminent relocation got channelled in a different direction, one that was in keeping with contemporary thinking about integration and public housing.

HALIFAX HUMAN RIGHTS ADVISORY COMMITTEE

In 1961, prior to the official establishment of the city's Development Department, Africville resident Joe Skinner was frustrated at not being able to secure a building permit to build a ranch-style bungalow on his land. Through his railway union contacts he sought advice from the Montreal office of the National Committee on Human Rights in the Canadian Labour Congress. He was advised, along with a handful of other Africvilleans who allied with him, to "organize the people of Africville into a group ... and ... press your case until the City takes remedial action." Subsequently a ratepayers association was formed whose core members were Joe Skinner, Leon and Emma Steed, deacons Mantley and Jones, and Harry Carter.

Association members, limited in resources, perceiving themselves without local allies and increasingly worried about the relocation threat, sought further assistance from the National Committee on Human Rights. In August 1962 the committee sent to Halifax "our best man in this field ... Alan Borovoy, a lawyer and our Ontario Human Rights Director ... [well-respected for] breaking down discrimination and obtaining

Leon and Emma Steed with granddaughter Bonnie.

anti-discrimination legislation in the housing field."

Borovoy travelled to Halifax from Toronto for a short visit and brought together the core members of the ratepayers association and a small group of white and black community leaders in the Halifax area. As a result, the Halifax Human Rights Advisory Committee (HHRAC) was formed with the tasks of assisting the Africville group and, as well, becoming active in advancing human rights legislation in employment and in housing. From this point on the fate of Africville and its response was inextricably linked to HHRAC.

At that time, in Canada and the United States, there was not only an optimism about government programs

Deacon George Mantley speaking at the public meeting.

of urban renewal, but also a strong civil rights movement emphasizing individual rights and freedoms and opposing racial segregation, unfair housing and employment practices.

Alan Borovoy was one of the leading proponents of civil liberties in Canada. It is not surprising that he would emphasize that a "black ghetto should not be subsidized" and that he would stress the importance of racial integration. From the outset he would see Africville in the context of the larger struggle for civil rights in Nova Scotia and elsewhere in North America.

Like Professor Stephenson, he had little appreciation of Africville's history and of its value as a community. He perceived Africville to be a slum and relocation to be virtually inevitable. Since his organization had no resources to commit to Africville and since his contacts indicated that Africvilleans had no strong power base from which to bargain, he considered that the best strategy for Africville was to develop an organization of influential Blacks and Whites which could be an important support for them.

This same basic thinking appears to have been shared by most core non-Africville members of the new Human Rights Committee, all of whom had a record of significant involvement in the human rights field. Strongly opposed to segregation and discrimination, they considered the relocation of the residents to be inevitable and saw their role as assisting Africvilleans get the best possible deal from the City. There was some recognition, especially but not only by the black members, that Africville was a community, not just a collection of people. At the same time, they had little familiarity with Africville's people or history and most perceived the community resourceless and slum-like.

Although seventy-one persons attended meetings of the Halifax Human Rights Advisory Committee (HHRAC) over the time it dealt with Africville, the core non-Africville members numbered seven, four Whites (two educators, a businessman and a union leader) and three Blacks (a principal, a lawyer and a minister). None of the local area's elected politicians, at any of the three levels of government, took on a role.

Few Africville residents were involved either.

The HHRAC met forty times between 1962 and 1967 but only five Africville residents attended more than two of these meetings, seven of which were held in Africville's Seaview Church. The chief Africville participants were the Steeds and Harry Carter. The Steeds in particular were widely respected in Africville as a caring, friendly couple who could articulate the community's concerns. Still, even they had no mandate to represent the whole of Africville. They largely acted as go-betweens to the community for HHRAC and others and themselves called no meetings of Africville residents.

Once HHRAC came on the scene, it became the only channel used for Africville-City contact regarding relocation plans and related considerations. Subsequently only one formal meeting of Africville residents was held outside HHRAC auspices. In October 1962 a meeting called by the Nova Scotia Association for the Advancement of Coloured Persons, chaired by Rev. W. Oliver and attended by some thirty Africville residents, was held at the Seaview Church. Published accounts indicate that the participants discussed the relocation question and concluded that under the circumstances relocation was almost inevitable and therefore emphasis should be placed on bargaining for the best terms possible.

Within two months of the large public meeting where most if not all Africvilleans present indicated their rejection of the City's plans to relocate them, relocation was deemed to be "almost inevitable" by the residents as well as their advocates. It would appear that the basis for independent community action was quite limited and that outside allies could not be convinced of the community's viability. From here on, HHRAC's core non-Africville members became, in effect, the community's representatives. They focused on obtaining better terms and compensation for the residents. While the involvement of these committee members did not cause any basic alteration in the Development Department's plans about Africville, it did result in the subsequent relocation requiring a great deal more of City money and staff time than anticipated.

Throughout the fall of 1962 and the whole of 1963 the HHRAC pursued various relocation issues with both Africville residents (basically the handful identified above) and City staff (basically the Development Department). HHRAC conveyed the concerns and

Buddy Daye.

questions which Africvilleans and others had to the Director of the Development Department who in turn provided written responses to the committee. As represented in documents of the HHRAC, Africville residents were specifically concerned with getting a "house for a house," with meeting the costs, financial and otherwise, of new housing arrangements and in obtaining a fair deal for their property. More generally, they and the HHRAC members wondered about the value of the land for industrial purposes and whether there was any alternative to the individual household relocation plan being suggested.

The responses of the Development Department were businesslike, rational and devoid of any sense of responsibility to Africville or any special obligation on the City's part. The City said that while the area was designated for industrial usage no such plan was imminent. It said that there was no alternative to individual household relocation since the costs for bringing Africville up to City specification would be over $800,000. City officials claimed that the City

Above: Seaview Church with children crossing the train tracks in the foreground.
Opposite: Meeting on relocation at church: Joe Skinner, B. A. Husbands and George Mantley.

would find it too costly and even morally objection-able (i.e. segregationist) to recreate Africville elsewhere in the City.

HHRAC members were assured that all Africville residents would be offered accommodation in public housing and that there was no realistic alternative to the kind of relocation envisaged by the City staff.

In May 1963 the HHRAC arranged for City staff to attend a public meeting at the Seaview Church and clarify City policy to Africvilleans. The meeting was quiet and ignited few sparks of protest. The HHRAC members were still somewhat anxious and uncertain about City claims that the demolition and relocation plan was the best or the only option for Africville. They decided to recommend to City Council that one of the leading advocates in the field of housing, urban renewal and social welfare, Dr. Albert Rose of the University of Toronto, be invited to come to Halifax to advise on the Africville situation. Rose had been involved in recent urban renewal programs where

Like them, he also felt that he could not recommend a segregated community, even a modern one, to replace what was there. Although very limited in his knowledge of the community, he considered that action and certainly not an in-depth study was required. Moreover, he believed that Africville residents and community leaders (presumably HHRAC and others) agreed that the community should be cleared. Indeed, in his report to Council a few weeks later, Rose contended that the residents of Africville were "ready and eager to negotiate," that community leaders agreed it was a slum and that it would have been cleared a long time ago "if the inhabitants were of a different racial background." Rose, in effect, endorsed the City's proposed plan, namely to negotiate terms with the residents for relocation, without any consideration to retaining the community.

The Rose report recommended that Africville be cleared over a two- to three-year period, and the residents receive not only better housing but also employment assistance and training, compensation for furniture and equipment needs, generous welfare assistance and free legal aid. Further, the report recommended that the HHRAC be involved in designing and monitoring the relocation and that a trained social worker, operating out of the Development Department, be hired to document the needs of each Africville household.

the solution to the problems of low-income housing involved relocation of residents into public housing complexes.

Rose visited Halifax on November 24-26, 1963. He discussed the Africville situation with City officials, university specialists, professional social workers and members of the HHRAC. His contact with Africville was limited to two hours touring the community in the company of City officials and to meeting once with the Africville members of HHRAC.

As with Professor Stephenson and Alan Borovoy, Rose was convinced that relocation was inevitable, that Africville conditions were deplorable and that rehabilitation of the community would be too costly.

The Rose report was praised by the local media and by City staff. The HHRAC voted unanimously to accept the recommendations of the report and on January 9, 1964 at a meeting in Africville, called by HHRAC, thirty-seven of the forty-one Africvilleans present voted to accept it. One week later City Council unanimously adopted the Rose report in principle and set up a special committee composed of members of Council, City staff and members of HHRAC to advise Council concerning implementation of the report.

IMPLEMENTING THE RELOCATION

Every year, as long as I can remember, I can remember them coming out there and surveying land and surveying all over the place. And the next thing that you know you see in the paper is where they are going to root Africville out, bulldoze Africville out. (Africville resident, 1969)

The emphasis was on the fact it was a social problem. So finally the then City fathers in 1961-62 ... attempted to do something for these people who were in the community of Africville and were considered to be disadvantaged people. (Relocation Social Worker, 1969)

Africville survived for well over a hundred years in spite of City policy and actions. Understandably, then, few residents believed at the time of relocation or later that the City's motives in the early sixties were to assist Africvilleans in any significant way. Certainly the City's historical position was that the lands would ultimately be required for industrial purposes and there were such plans under consideration at the time. Supported by the Stephenson and Rose reports, the official reason for the relocation was the poor quality of Africville housing.

In implementing the relocation program, the City basically followed the policies recommended by Rose. The program was coordinated by the Department of Development. A trained social worker employed by the Province, Peter MacDonald, was seconded to the City for three years. He was charged with visiting and documenting the social and economic situation and requirements of each family and guiding all Africville residents through the relocation process. Regular meetings between him and the Director of Development established the basis for each negotiation with individual residents, which were then carried out by the relocation social worker.

In general there were two types of "compensation" — compensation for land and buildings, and assistance in starting anew elsewhere. The latter, as Rose specified, was especially to entail generous welfare assistance for as long as required, employment and educational rehabilitation, and help in securing better housing accommodations. Apart from property settlements, the relocation social worker was the main authority in new housing arrangements, welfare assistance and furniture money.

In keeping with Rose's recommendation, the HHRAC continued to have a significant role in the relocation process. Initially reports detailing settlements were passed on to the City Council's Subcommittee on Africville then to HHRAC before being formally submitted to City Council for ratification. Later the

A view of Big Town.

procedure was streamlined when these two bodies merged to form a new Subcommittee on Africville with three Council representatives and three black non-Africville representatives from HHRAC.

Once a settlement was reached with each party, Peter MacDonald's report would be submitted to the Subcommittee, then to Council's Finance Committee and finally to Council as a whole. There were very few cases where the social worker's reports were contested, though initially there was more independent checking carried out by the HHRAC representatives. Once the relocation process began there was no significant formal involvement of any Africvilleans. HHRAC acted as if it were an arm of the City bureaucracy. It was given powers by the City and expected to look after Africvilleans' interests; in return, its involvement stamped the relocation program as progressive and humane.

Although the key person in the relocation process was the Director of Development, the relocation social worker was the main contact for residents. A forty-year-old Cape Bretoner, Peter MacDonald exhibited some empathy with Africvilleans and appreciated their long struggle, and he was able to win the trust of most residents. He spent most of the first six months (i.e. June to December 1964) meeting the residents informally in their homes and on the roads. His perception was that the community was quite divided in its views about the program and that there were five or six groups of residents.

The relocation social worker spent most time initially with those Africvilleans who had participated in HHRAC and with influential residents who were at least somewhat willing to move. He also visited frequently with the Big Town area residents whom he sympathized with and admired because of their resourceful if somewhat rebellious and deviant lifestyle. Relatively little time was spent with the young adults, presumably because here the critical relocation aspect was not property settlement but programs to effect new life opportunities, an aspect that in practice was accorded low priority. Comparatively little time also was spent with stubborn and resistant residents.

The adult renters received the least attention since the relocation social worker shared the view of many Africvilleans and even these persons themselves, namely that they did not really belong to Africville; indeed, asked how he dealt with one white transient, Peter MacDonald replied: "I informed him of his rights as a citizen." The City strategy was to remove as soon as possible those willing to relocate, quickly demolish their dwellings and sheds and thereby underline the fact that the demolition of the community was well under way.

Despite, or perhaps because of, the long-standing threat of relocation, most Africville residents indicated that they were surprised when they realized that relocation actually was going to happen. Approximately forty per cent of the adults interviewed in 1968–69, roughly two years after their relocation, indicated that they were very or somewhat willing to relocate upon becoming aware of the relocation program.

Many residents were confident that they could negotiate a good deal for their property while younger household heads hoped that the relocation rhetoric would be realized for themselves in new opportunities. The tenants, mostly older adults without families, realistically saw themselves as outsiders without any claims, non-participants in the relocation business who accepted the "inconvenient" relocation in an unemotional fashion and simply hoped for a good deal. Elderly long-time residents clearly exhibited the greatest grief and the most reluctance to relocate.

THE COST OF RELOCATION

There was little community organization developed around the relocation. There were no general community meetings held to discuss the relocation

independently of those called by HHRAC and other outside officials. The negotiation structure reduced the chances of a collective action by Africville residents. The arrangement implied that professionals were looking after relocatees' interests and that little could be gained by community mobilization.

The style of relocation negotiation by Africvilleans was "everyone for himself," tempered by various strategies to assist close family members. Significant suspicion and jealousy developed, partly because of the complications of land ownership claims (only fourteen residents had clear legal title to their property) and partly because of the secrecy and diversity of the specific settlement packages arranged through the relocation social worker. The City's strategy to settle with some influential residents and quickly demolish their properties yielded the anticipated results.

There were "community leaders" who were going to represent the people of Africville against the City ... The first thing you know [these leaders] ... are the first ones to move. Well! When we saw them leaving, we all figured that what's the sense of staying if the leaders of the rest of us are gone.

Residents differed in how actively they set about trying to get the best deal for themselves and their families in the relocation negotiations, from those who took an active part, to those who resigned themselves to the decisions of the social worker/negotiator. Some of the older residents set what they considered a high price and refused to budge or to enter into any negotiations at all. Very few Africvilleans used any outside assistance such as HHRAC members or free City legal and real estate services. A handful reported contact with other local black leaders for assistance during the relocation process. Essentially, Africvilleans depended upon their own resources and their relationship with the relocation social worker.

The actual relocation took place essentially between 1964 and 1967, beginning within a month of the social worker taking up his duties. The first deal involved a woman who sold her house (she did not own the land) and received $500, free moving, accommodation in public housing and the cancellation of an outstanding $1500 hospital bill. The settlement was deemed fair by HHRAC, which had undertaken an independent appraisal of the property.

Halifax Human Rights Advisory Committee meeting with Alan Borovoy at the Halifax Hotel.

All told, the City spent about $550,000 for the Africville lands and the buildings; another $200,000 was budgeted (up to 1969) for welfare assistance, furniture allowance and the waiving of unpaid taxes and hospital bills. The trustees of the Seaview Church accepted an offer of $15,000 for the church building and the money was deposited in an education trust fund to be used for Blacks in the Halifax area, with preference to be given to children of Africville relocatees.

City expenditure far exceeded the Development Department's 1961 estimate of $70,000. In fact the total costs approximated $800,000, the figure that City officials earlier deemed prohibitively high for the alternative of bringing Africville up to standard in terms of City services and housing quality. Unlike most urban renewal projects, the City did not receive nor seek federal funding for the acquisition and clearance of Africville properties, as the National Housing Act provided for compensation only where legal title was unquestioned.

While the relocation plans had called for educational and occupational programs and the creation of new and better life opportunities for the relocated people, virtually nothing happened along these lines. Relocatees were directed to existing programs or services. After residents had been relocated, there was almost no follow-up. The social worker, the only person assigned to this, was too occupied with negotiations and rehousing.

Black and white members of HHRAC and the special Africville subcommittee expressed shock upon learning that there had been no follow-up in 1968. One noted, "I assumed there was a follow-up.... I didn't know that these people were just left completely to their own resources.... I should have known but I didn't."

Africville residents had no direct way, as a group, to bargain or to call attention to shortfalls in the program. HHRAC members were concerned activists, but as volunteers they had limited time and resources and depended largely on the reports of the relocation social worker. He, in turn, had little time to pursue

Above and left: City truck and movers moving Dorothy Carvery.

new programs and also had to balance the interests of Africvilleans with the City's concern for quick clearance at modest costs. The conflict of interest in the social worker's situation does not seem to have been a matter of concern at the time. Finally, because the goals and objectives of the program remained vague, success was difficult to gauge in any event.

The benefits of relocation fell far short of the promises in other respects as well. City staff sometimes moved relocatees to run-down, decrepit City-owned housing slated for redevelopment. A number of Africvilleans also complained about being moved in "big yellow city trucks." As one relocatee declaimed, "City people sent a truck to move my furniture. Just think what the neighbours thought when they looked out and saw a garbage truck drive up and unload the furniture."

Promises and understandings in the settlement packages were often neither fully authorized nor written down and they became points of contention later when the relocation social worker's job ended in 1967.

Above: Uncle Jimmy Dixon.
Right: Dorothy Carvery.

Finally the relocation itself ended on a sour note when expropriation threats and intimidation were used to get the last Africville resident, "Pa" Carvery, to come to terms. Construction work on a new bridge was being delayed because its Halifax base was to be built on his property. The delay was proving costly to the City so Carvery was summoned to City Hall in December 1969 and, in the presence of several top City staff, shown a suitcase filled with money. He related the incident as follows:

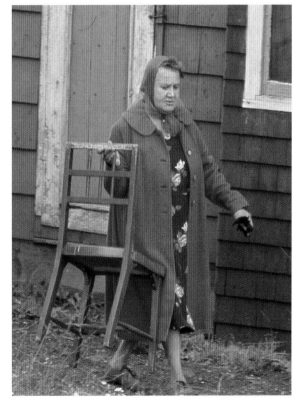

> *They sent for me and when I got there I was taken into someone's office. There was five or six people in the room [actually there was the City solicitor, the director of finance, the internal auditor, the social planner, the Africville Special Projects Officer and two plainclothes officers] plus a suitcase full of money tied up neatly in bundles.... The suitcase was open and stuck under my nose so as to tempt me and try to pay me off right then and there.... I didn't like it*

at all.... It hurt me.... I told them, "You guys think you're smart.... well, you're not smart enough," then I got up and walked out of the office.

On January 2, 1970, Carvery, the last holdout, having reluctantly reached an agreement with the City, vacated his premises. Four days later his building was bulldozed.

Of course, well before this the relocation organization had been dismantled. Peter MacDonald had returned to Cape Breton. Members of HHRAC had turned their attention to provincial legislation and organization. The Department of Development had turned its attention to the Halifax waterfront. Africvilleans were again on their own.

THE INITIAL IMPACT OF RELOCATION

Despite the substantial failure of the relocation promise, many Africville residents, especially the young adults with families and individuals without strong community ties, were initially satisfied with the settlement they received from the City. Young families usually received enough to make a new beginning — furniture allowance, social assistance and public housing units. Those who had neither property nor high expectations were often satisfied with trivial settlements, such as a few hundred dollars, some short-term welfare and rental accommodation in the City's redevelopment area. Those with bargaining power because of property ownership considered that they were able to get what they wanted in their negotiations with the relocation social worker. Older residents with deep roots in the community were most likely to be dissatisfied even when they perceived themselves as obtaining a fair deal in the negotiations. One person observed:

I suppose I got a fair deal but we'll be in debt for the rest of our lives. I'd sooner be back in Africville. I owned my own home there. I got mortgage payments to meet here.

Housing in Halifax was in short supply and the scale of urban renewal being undertaken in these years made it difficult for families and individuals in need to secure public housing. Racism made the housing situation more difficult for Blacks. Just prior to the relocation and on the basis of a rumour that public housing for Africvilleans was to be constructed in a certain area, some Whites arranged a protest with the message, "We don't want Africville people here." And during the relocation there were two instances of white neighbours harassing Africville relocatees who purchased homes.

Nevertheless, by most criteria the quality of the new housing was better for most relocatees. Twenty-eight families and seven unattached individuals obtained public housing units while twenty-four family heads became homeowners. Generally these relocatees appreciated the better facilities, services and conveniences. In some instances of home ownership there was a sense of quite complete satisfaction. For example, one relocated resident observed:

My children, they come to visit me and they like the home and hate going back to Montreal. This is an ideal place for an old couple to retire. We have all the conveniences. The neighbourhood is friendly and the scenery is beautiful. We have to pay twice as much now to live; we have the same amount of money coming in as we had in Africville but it's well worth it.

Relocatees who were in other rental situations, some fifty-five adults and ten families, fared less well with their new accommodations, much of which was substandard and slated for demolition.

Africville residents typically relocated in the north and central areas of Halifax, not too far from the Africville site. Most were quite familiar with their new neighbourhood, did not feel out of place there and maintained close contacts with their former Africville friends.

AFTER RELOCATION

The costs of relocation were significant, and for many they increased as time went on. With better housing came increased expenditure for mortgage/rent, fuel and the like. To people underemployed, without adequate and regular income, unused to such expenditures, this improved housing brought new worries, family strains and indebtedness.

Since there had been no effective employment or education program, the relocatees soon became very dependent upon social assistance. More than half of the

Aaron (Pa) Carvery, the last resident to leave Africville.

relocatee households regularly received City or provincial welfare, whereas prior to relocation, no more than ten per cent had done so.

The financial pressures were very onerous for homeowners, especially among those whose relocation settlement was modest or who lacked regular employment. Within two years, five such homeowners had lost their new homes and several others were threatened with a similar fate.

With public housing came bureaucratic rules affecting valued life styles; one relocatee noted, "I wanted one of my grandsons (fifteen years old) to move in with me but that would have been an extra thirty dollars a month. So that would have been too much money to pay."

Interviewed in 1969, the majority of relocatees — about 70 per cent — reported having suffered personal crises as a consequence of relocation and having trouble making ends meet. The initial satisfaction of many relocatees waned as the short-term nature of benefits, e.g. furniture allowance, welfare, sympathetic attention of City officials, became apparent. Moreover, many relocatees found that different City bureaucrats challenged unwritten agreements they had had with the social worker concerning rental subsidy and social assistance.

On the whole, Africvilleans had become more vulnerable to money problems, more beholden to others' rules (public housing or welfare authorities) and less enmeshed in family and community support systems. Further, many had lost their main bargaining chip, their property, and as one man said with grief, "I will die and won't be able to leave my children anything." Small wonder then that 95 per cent of the relocatees thought that the City got the best of the "relocation deal" and even 80 per cent felt that they personally did not get "a good deal" from the City.

As the City became aware of the problems through the requests to Social Planning for assistance in the form of advice and welfare benefits, their response was to encourage the organization of a committee — the Committee of Former Africville Residents — which led shortly thereafter to the creation of the Seaview Credit Union in 1968.

The modestly funded Credit Union (the Province contributed $50,000 and the City $20,000, all of which was supposed to be repayable) was to be managed and controlled by former Africville residents in collaboration with Social Planning staff. While the Credit Union was providing short-term help to those in pressing need, more attention was to be directed at long-term solutions of employment, housing and education.

Within a year and a half this post-relocation program lay in ruins. The Credit Union funds were largely disbursed and there was little hope of much repayment, in part because the recipients had no means for doing so and in part because disgruntled relocatees considered the loan money to be relocation compensation.

The other long-term plans for educational and employment benefits were so modest as to be virtually irrelevant.

In the late summer of 1969, the former Africville residents formed their own Africville Action Committee. Led initially by relocatees who were pragmatic and dissatisfied less with the fact of relocation than with the terms of the relocation "exchange," this group was hoping to get more direct compensation. With wide Africville support, the organization lobbied for more just property settlements, in effect, a final overall government payment that would constitute an emergency fund for the relocated residents.

Over the next two years the committee mobilized support among other City organizations, wrote letters to the newspapers and met with the mayor and City council. The lack of resources and experienced leaders coupled with the bureaucratic and legal objections to proposals, and the passivity, if not cool response of local politicians, ultimately caused the Action Committee to wear down and fade away. However, it did spawn,

with Social Planning, a few marginally useful programs such as a special employment training project in which a handful of relocatees participated. And it was instrumental in arranging an appropriate ceremony of remembrance for the old Africville community.

On Sunday, August 6, 1972 twelve hundred persons, young and old, gathered on the Africville site for a spiritual revival and memorial service; it was an honourable event for a unique community.

AFRICVILLE AS A SYMBOL

At the time of relocation many non-Africville Blacks shared the wider society's negative conception of Africville and supported the relocation program. Black leaders, aware of the causes of Africville's peculiar development (especially the racism), expressed hope that the residents would be treated fairly and generously. Some leaders called for the construction of a new, serviced Africville community, but most black leaders did not explicitly adopt this view. Rather, they emphasized that the relocation should bring real opportunity for the families and individuals relocated in an integrationist context.

Apart from the black members of the HHRAC, there was little involvement in the relocation by Blacks outside Africville. Moreover, Africvilleans apparently did not seek support in the broader black community.

The climate of opinion at the time emphasized civil rights and integration rather than the celebration of the black community in itself and the articulation of the black experience in Nova Scotia. In metropolitan Halifax some black spokesmen were impatient with what they viewed then as the inward, community-looking, traditional black leadership and were in sympathy with integration and the relocation program.

Since the relocation, however, Africville has become central in the new black consciousness in Nova Scotia. It has become something to appreciate and identify with. Africville has become a symbol of why black organization and solidarity are necessary to fight racism.

In the early 1970s, one prominent black leader indicated that when he went into a new community to organize the residents there, his message was "Let's pull together, or else we'll be another Africville" — a message that was proclaimed on many occasions in the following years.

There are several reasons for the considerable change in the perception of Africville and the relocation in

Joe Skinner.

the years immediately following the relocation. The shortfalls in the relocation program and the subsequent protests by Africvilleans alerted Blacks to the dangers of government-initiated change where there is neither adequate acknowledgement of racism nor sufficient opportunity for participation and advocacy. Black leaders also began to draw similarities between Africville and other black communities where deeds were in disarray, housing conditions poor and the land was becoming valuable for watershed, industrial and other purposes. Perhaps most importantly, there was the emergence of new cultural, organizational and political responses among black Nova Scotians; these were associated with the growth of black identity and pride, the promotion of unity among Blacks and an assertive, confrontational approach to racism and disadvantage.

New secular organizations have developed such as the Black United Front and the Afro-Canadian Liberation Movement. There has been a considerable increase in the number of black professionals — lawyers, teachers and social workers. A Human Rights Commission was set up by the provincial government after considerable pressure from black leaders. Black artists, writers and entertainers have put expression to a new mood in the black community. Indeed, the Africville experience has been credited by many observers as providing a stimulus for some of these developments. Certainly too, these developments have led to redefinitions of the Africville situation. As one leader observed "This [the Africville relocation] could not happen again."

Indeed it has not. Since Africville, black communities such as Beechville and North Preston, on the outskirts of Halifax-Dartmouth, have progressed through housing cooperatives and community development programs essentially under the control of their residents.

The symbolic significance of Africville goes beyond the black community. The wider Nova Scotian society has increasingly come to accept that the relocation broke up a community and did not provide an adequate substitute for the residents. The Africville experience has helped to clarify what community signifies — not housing, sewerage and so on, but identity, interdependence and need.

The Africville relocation has symbolic value as virtually the last large-scale relocation of people into public housing and the destruction of their community. Such

Cyril Cassidy, Stephen Mantley and Dorothy Carvery.

upheavals, common in the 1950s and 1960s, have since become discredited. The relocation, thanks to the social worker and the black members of HHRAC, did yield some benefits to some individuals but, like other urban renewal programs, it became largely a re-housing scheme with welfare payments added to ease the transition.

THE LEGACY OF AFRICVILLE

Where Africville once stood there is now an under-utilized park that comes to life each summer when the Africville Genealogical Society holds its reunion weekend there. A member of the society explained its objective as follows:

The reunion is important to the descendants because it gives them a place to come back to and remember. And it is important to teach the children.... We hope that they can learn from what has happened. (Interview, 1986)

There is still some organization among Africvilleans and the last line has not been written as far as the land usage is concerned. The negative stereotype of Africville has been laid to rest and the initial City and media claims of a progressive relocation have been debunked. Asked to reflect on Africville, one older relocatee in 1969 stated, simply,

Africville was a place where many coloured people lived together trying to do the best they could.

Africville lives on as an indictment against racism, as a critique of technocratic, imposed approaches to social change, and as a celebration of community and the human spirit. Forty-one years ago, the local news-paper proclaimed, "Soon Africville will be but a name. And in the not too distant future that too, mercifully, will be forgotten." It hasn't been. It shouldn't be. It won't be.

CHAPTER 4

THE AFRICVILLE EXPERIENCE:
LESSONS FOR THE FUTURE

STEPHEN KIMBER

Africville reunion, 1984.

DR. BRIDGLAL PACHAI: Good evening, ladies and gentlemen. I would like to welcome you to "The Africville Experience: Lessons for the Future." May I begin by calling upon Reverend Charles Coleman, onetime pastor of the Seaview Baptist Church in Africville, to say a prayer.

REVEREND CHARLES COLEMAN: Our Father and Our God, we come before Thy presence tonight to deal with serious matters, matters that not only affect our lives today but in the future. And as we gather together we ask Thy presence with us, Thy blessing upon this gathering and upon those issues that we are considering and dealing with. May Thy guidance and — most of all — may Thy hope be among us. Amen.

More than 150 people — young, old, black, white, powerful, powerless, decision-makers and those who have endured the consequences of their decisions — have gathered tonight in a small auditorium at Mount Saint Vincent University in Halifax.

They are here to try to come to terms with what one participant will describe as "something terrible" that happened more than twenty-five years ago. Why did it happen? Could it have been prevented? Should it have been prevented? What can we learn from it now? What can — should — be done today to atone for that "something terrible" that happened and that now virtually everyone agrees should never have happened at all?

That "something terrible," of course, is the

Brenda Steed-Ross.

destruction of Africville, the small black community nestled on the edge of the Bedford Basin at the north end of the City of Halifax that was bulldozed into history during the late 1960s, in the name of the greater good of better housing, of integration, of progress.

No one who was involved in making the fateful decisions about Africville in the early 1960s would probably have ever imagined that people would still be debating the wisdom of their decisions in 1989. That they are is a tribute to the resilient spirit of the people of Africville, and to their own remarkable community organization, the Africville Genealogy Society. Although the society did not officially come into existence until 1983, its real beginnings go back twenty-five years earlier to a sweet summer afternoon in 1958 when eight-year-old Debbie Dixon[3] and her best friend, ten-year-old Brenda Steed, became blood sisters. "I remember we were sitting on the

well-platform in my yard and trying to work up our courage," Brenda Steed remembers with a laugh today. "We were so scared. Finally, we pricked our fingers just enough to get a little blood. We were so proud of ourselves. We were going to be blood sisters forever."

And they were. Even after relocation pushed their families in different directions, and little Debbie grew up to be Deborah Dixon-Jones and Brenda became Brenda Steed-Ross, they — along with their other best friend, Linda Mantley — remained as close as real sisters. "Every time we'd get together, sooner or later we'd end up talking about Africville," Brenda Steed recalls. "Debbie'd say, Brenda, remember when we were out home doing this, that or the other thing, and then we'd be off, talking and laughing and remembering."

But the comforting, day-to-day I'll-help-you-you-help-me sense of community they had shared with their friends and neighbours back in Africville all too

Above: First Africville reunion, 1972.
Right: Seaview Memorial Park, a National Historic Site.

soon became little more than memories. "It got so we'd never see anyone from out home unless it was at Christmastime or Easter, or if we happened to run into them at a funeral or a wedding," Steed-Ross says. "The ones who were children at the time of the relocation grew up and began having children of their own and we didn't even recognize them on the street. We felt like we were losing our identity."

By 1982, Dixon-Jones decided it was time that they did something to change all that. She, Steed-Ross and Mantley organized an "Acquaintance Day" so that former Africville residents could get together, reminisce about old times, meet their community's newest generation and, in the process, keep the spirit of Africville alive.

Where better to hold such an event than in Seaview Park, the recreation area that Halifax City had finally created out of their razed community? "Some of us had already started going out there on our own from time to time, just to have picnics or go fishing or whatever, so we could spend some time out home again," Brenda Steed-Ross remembers. "Even though all that was left was just a field, it still felt like being home. The school ground was still there and right over from that was the church. I knew where my house used to be because I always identified it with a certain pile of rocks. I could go to the very spot where my house used to be, and all

81

Above and right: Africville reunions run annually, attracting former residents and descendants.

sorts of memories would come back to me."

But Dixon-Jones was adamant that Acquaintance Day should be something more than a once-in-a-life-time weekend to wallow in a shared nostalgia for times that had gone. She wanted to create something that would keep the sense of community that was at the heart of the spirit of Africville alive for the generations still to come.

The result was the Africville Genealogy Society. "We went down to the Registry of Joint Stocks and incorporated ourselves as a society," Brenda Steed-Ross remembers. They elected a board of directors, established phone committees, held monthly meetings, organized tag days and Easter egg hunts and, of course, hosted the annual picnic and reunion each July in Seaview Park.

Like most other former residents of Africville, Irvine Carvery, who was fifteen when the bulldozers flattened his parents' home, went to the reunions — they brought back sweet memories for him too — but he didn't become active in the organization itself at first.

"When it was getting started," he explains now, "I was busy with other things, and the society didn't seem interested in the issues that I was. They saw the society as a way of keeping the traditions alive, but I thought we needed to become more political."

Carvery went to Halifax City Council on his own to demand that the City not only apologize to the former residents of Africville for taking their land but also allow them to return to Africville and re-establish their community. "The City listened to me but nothing happened," Carvery recalls. "My presentation went to the basement or wherever those things go."

But his ideas intrigued and attracted the interest — and support — of many former Africville residents, all of whom felt they'd been the victims of a terrible injustice. They elected him the fourth president of the Africville Genealogy Society.[4] Carvery is quick to point out that his election didn't mean a split in the Genealogy Society — "At the same time I was elected president, Linda Mantley was elected vice-president, so we're combining interest in maintaining the traditions with the recognition that we have to fight for what's rightfully ours." Carvery's philosophy is simple. "I think you can't maintain the traditions and show respect for the elders of the community without being political," he says. "If you want to respect the elders you've got to fight for what they believed in and what

Opening ceremony, Seaview Memorial Park.

they believed in was that the people of Africville should never have been moved."

That may help explain why Carvery was enthusiastic when a group — including Mary Sparling, the director of the Art Gallery, Mount Saint Vincent University, Shelagh Mackenzie, a National Film Board producer, Bridglal Pachai, the director of the Nova Scotia Black Cultural Society (and later executive director of the Nova Scotia Human Rights Commission), Henry Bishop, Curator of the Black Cultural Centre, and Don Clairmont, a Dalhousie University sociologist who had written a seminal book about the Africville relocation — approached him in 1988 to see if the Genealogy Society might be interested in becoming involved in organizing an exhibition about Africville. Mackenzie, who had collaborated with Sparling on an earlier exhibition, "A Black Community Album," organized with the Mount gallery, told him that she'd been hearing about Africville ever since she moved to Nova Scotia in 1973 and wanted to learn more about the community.

For the Africville Genealogical Society, on the other hand, the exhibition was a chance to finally make the point to their broader community that Africville — a place that many Whites still associated with stereotyped images of slums and ghettos — was a living, breathing, sharing, caring community. And also to make their case that Africville's former residents and their descendants deserved some form of compensation for the wrong that had been done to them.

Over the next year-and-a-half, an organizing committee began collecting artefacts — fine china and linens, old photos, a pulpit rescued from the ruins of the Seaview Church — that eventually gave the exhibition its wonderfully "homey" sense of community and put the lie to those still far too widely held stereotypes of what Africville was like.

If an exhibition about a particular community seemed an unusual undertaking for an art gallery, so too was the official opening that launched the show in Halifax in October 1989. This opening began with a moving service of dedication at Cornwallis Street Baptist Church, the "mother" church for Africville's Seaview Baptist Church, in the heart of what is now

Musician Joe Sealy and his father.

Halifax's black community. Cornwallis Street's pastor, Reverend J.C. Mack, even invited well-known black clergymen Donald Skeir, the pastor of the East Preston Baptist Church, to deliver a special sermon to mark the occasion.

"The leaders of our land can go all across this world talking about human rights, but let us never forget the black people in a community called Africville," Reverend Skeir told the mixed black and white congregation in a sermon that was punctuated by "Amens" and applause. "They too were oppressed and depressed. But they have survived because they have that spirit within them that has motivated our people for 300 years."

Amen.

That same spirit was very much in evidence at Mount Saint Vincent University's Seton Auditorium later in November during a vibrant evening of rhythm and readings staged to celebrate the exhibition. Between Lucky Campbell's dramatic readings from the essay by writer Charles Saunders that describes life in Africville in all its many textures, and a poetry reading by Dartmouth poet Maxine Tynes, a host of almost exclusively black musicians — including Africville's own Flint Family and the West sisters, as well as Faith Nolan, Preston's Gospel Heirs, the Cobequid Road Baptist Church Brotherhood, Joe Sealy, Bucky Adams and Four the Moment (a Halifax a cappella group who'd once turned down an invitation to sing for Canada's housing ministers because organizers insisted they drop a song about Africville from their repertoire) — celebrated the community's enduring spirit in song.

The idea to have a conference in conjunction with the exhibition "just sort of evolved out of our discussions," Irvine Carvery remembered later. "It seemed like the logical extension of the exhibition."

It was. But it was more than that too. The Africville exhibition opened at a time when Nova Scotians were finally beginning to deal with a long-festering but rarely acknowledged reality — the racism in their own society.

Two years of hearings by a provincial royal commission looking into the wrongful conviction of a young Native named Donald Marshall, Jr. had cast the unforgiving glare of publicity on a judicial system that seemed to treat people differently depending on their race and social status.

More recently, Nova Scotians had been shocked

Opening of the Africville exhibition, October 20, 1989.

THE AFRICVILLE EXPERIENCE
LESSONS FOR THE FUTURE
A CONFERENCE, HIGHLIGHTED BY THREE MAJOR PANELS, FREE AND OPEN TO THE PUBLIC, IN CONJUNCTION WITH THE EXHIBITION

Africville — A Spirit That Lives On

Auditorium C, Seton Academic Centre Mount Saint Vincent
University Halifax, Nova Scotia
17 and 18 November, 1989
8 pm Friday, 17 November

The Decision Makers: Why They Did What They Did,
chaired by Carolyn Thomas, African United Baptist Association, brings together some of the key players in the decisions taken between 1964 and 1970
10 am Saturday, 18 November

The Africville Response: How It Felt Then and How It Feels Now,
presents a range of voices from within the community, chaired by Brenda Steed-Ross, a founding member of the Africville Genealogy Society
1:20 pm Saturday, 18 November

A presentation by the Honourable Ronald Giffin, Minister of Education for Nova Scotia
1:30 pm Saturday, 18 November

Lessons From the Experience,
recommendations for change by people affected in various ways, chaired by the Reverend Charles Coleman, a former Africville pastor

Organized by the Africville Genealogy Society, the Black Cultural Centre for Nova Scotia, the Art Gallery, Mount Saint Vincent University, and the National Film Board, Atlantic Centre
Supported by Air Canada, City of Dartmouth, Moosehead Breweries Ltd., L. E. Shaw Ltd., and Jean Shaw
Lunch will be available in the Seton Centre Lobby for $3.00.
Call 443 4450 for further information.

by a series of well-publicized, racially-charged fights between black and white students at Cole Harbour District High School near Dartmouth. The fights — and the soul-searching that followed them — raised even more questions about what was wrong with relations between Blacks and Whites in the province.

After the confrontations, a group of parents and students at the school got together to demand the provincial government launch a broad public inquiry into the role of racism in Nova Scotia society. The government refused. At first, some government ministers actually insisted there was no racism in Nova Scotia. By the time Nova Scotia Education Minister Ron Giffin spoke to this Africville "Lessons for the Future" conference some months later, however, he admitted that racism was indeed a fact of life in Nova Scotia.

"Having grown up in Nova Scotia in Windsor and living now in Truro, I am as aware as anyone of the racism that exists in our society," he told those attending the conference.

Despite his admission, Giffin insisted the government did not need to appoint a royal commission or a public inquiry to look into this now-obvious truth. "We learned a great deal from what happened in Africville with respect to what we're now doing in North Preston," he explained. "The things that are

Sunday school class.

being done there today — the services that are being put in, the housing, the new elementary school that's going to be built — those are things that should have been done in Africville. We all know that. But quite frankly, I don't need to spend millions of dollars on an inquiry to find out what I already know. Racism exists in our society. And there in no quick fix to racism," he added. "It takes time and effort. And it's not just the job of government to solve the problem. It's society's problem, so it's really a question of what are we all going to do about it?"

This was the backdrop against which the more than 150 people gathered at Mount Saint Vincent University in November 1989 to talk about what lessons they could learn for the future from the "something terrible" that had happened not a mile from where the conference was being held.

Mount Saint Vincent University, in fact, was an ironically appropriate place for such an exhibition and conference to take place. The fact that you could look across Bedford Basin from the Mount's campus and see the site of what used to be Africville was just one of many connections between the university and the community of Africville. The Sisters of Charity, the religious order that once ran the Mount, used to send its sisters to teach arts and crafts to youngsters at Africville's community school. At the same time, men and women from Africville headed in the other direction to work in the Mount's kitchens and residences. As often as not, the women were paid with food rather than money.

Now a few of them and their sons and daughters — along with others from all segments of the Nova Scotian community — were coming together to talk through the questions of why Africville had been destroyed, whether what happened then could happen today and, perhaps most importantly for the former residents of Africville, what should be done now to put things right for the people whose lives had been so dramatically altered by events in which they had had no say.

For those who had not lived through — or been directly affected by — the relocation, the weekend's most moving moments came during a panel featuring members of the Africville Genealogy Society talking about how they felt about the relocation at the time that it happened and how they feel today, more than 25 years later.

Irvine Carvery was just 15 when the bulldozers came to raze his home. Today he is the Halifax Regional School Board Chair as well as the president of the Africville Genealogy Society.

IRVINE CARVERY: I was young when we lived in Africville and, to me at that time, Africville was my universe — just the Basin and the hills around and Africville. We didn't travel too much out of our community other than to go back and forth to our school.

I remember a time when I was out picking blueberries with Terry [Dixon] and I fell down on a bottle and cut my hand. Well, I didn't have to go all the way back home to have my cut mended. I went to the very first house that was there and I was taken care of. That was one of the things that was very important to me as a person living in Africville — the closeness and the oneness of the people.

You weren't isolated at any time living in Africville, you always felt at home, the doors were always open. That is one of the most important things that has stayed with me throughout my life.

The other part of living in Africville was the freedom that we had there — we had open fields, we had forested areas, we had the water. Recreation was at our fingertips. You weren't encumbered by people with restrictions, the way you felt in the city.

I remember the church and the important part it played in our lives. You had to go to Sunday School or else you were in big trouble. Deacon Jones was right down the road and he played the music on Sunday, so you didn't go near his house if you didn't go to Sunday School. If Deacon Mantley saw you, he would either give you a clip on the side of the head, or you'd be told pretty good that you were expected to be in Sunday School every Sunday.

I also remember the social worker coming to Africville, spending time in my grandmother's house. My grandmother was the postmistress in Africville, and a lot of the community things centred at her house, because everyone came there to pick up their mail. I remember asking my grandmother, "Who is this man and what are you talking about?" She told me, "This is a social worker from Halifax and they are talking about moving Africville." My question was,

Irvine Carvery.

"Well, why? Why do we have to go?"

Being as young as I was, I didn't feel the full impact of the move, or didn't have a realization of what it meant. I was excited about the move because it was something new and, being young, you look forward to anything that's new.

I remember my first bad experience involving the relocation of Africville. We used to have a little shed that no one used anymore, so us young guys used it as a hangout, and sometimes we used to spend the night there. I remember this one morning we were in there and a bulldozer was coming through it, and the wall was coming down. Now, that was my first real experience with relocation. The relocation process itself stems from that — there was no feeling for the people, there was no consideration for the people's feelings. We were lucky to be able to get out of there. We could

Laura Howe.

have been killed. They didn't check to see if there was anybody in there, they just assumed. A lot of things that happened with the relocation of our community were based on assumptions.

That is how I feel today. I am older now and able to look back. We are able now to look back on these events and make our own decisions and make our own value judgments on what happened. Today I feel just as strongly as I felt then.

My other strongest memory of the relocation of Africville is my grandmother crying because she had to leave her home. My grandmother and a lot of other people of Africville did not want to leave their community. A long tradition of people, of family and heritage is in the community and we did not want to leave. She cried when she had to leave, she was never happy after she left. I believe the relocation took away five years, minimum, from the lives of our loved ones,

of our elders.

Those are the feelings that I still feel today, and I feel very strongly about that. I feel that it was a complete injustice. I don't feel that the city dealt on an equal basis with the people of the community of Africville.

The people of Africville, as far as I am concerned, were not represented in any meetings for anything. These decisions were made without the input of the people of Africville.

So, that is how I feel today, the same way I felt back then, only now I have a broader perspective on the experience, and to me the experience was a negative one. I hope to continue fighting so that the people of Africville receive their just due from the City of Halifax and the people of Halifax.

Laura Howe was a mother raising her family in Africville at the time the community was relocated.

LAURA HOWE: I come this morning sort of representing the older generation. To me that is very, very important, because we have the old and the young and the in-between, but we all work as one.

When I first heard about the relocation of Africville twenty-five years ago, I began to wonder why, and I'm still wondering why.

To me, one sad part of it was the moving of our church. Our church meant so much to us. It was the vocal and spiritual part of our lives in Africville. All over the community, we could hear that bell. How it would toll! To me it would just say, "Come to church." You could almost hear the words, "Come to church ... come to church," and I am sure that many of the people that lived out there have fond memories of the church. No matter where we go, we always say there will never, never, never be another church like that little Seaview Baptist Church out in Africville.

I remember my son coming home one night and he said, "Mom, the church is gone." This was about three or four o'clock in the morning, and I said, "Oh no, no, it can't be, it was there about a week or so ago, maybe two weeks." He said, "No, Mom, it is flat to the ground." It was done in the early hours in the morning. It seemed to me to be such a cruel thing to do to a church. I never really could understand why it was done. Then I thought, maybe that's why it was done when nobody was around.

When I realized that it was going through and that

First church service, 1972: Ardith Pye, Mae West, Laura Howe, Elsie Desmond, Althea Mantley.

we were to be removed from our homes and placed in the City of Halifax, I began to wonder what is going to happen to all of our people. We were a large community — about eighty families, three to four hundred people. I questioned in my mind, where are we all going?

But we had to go on and try to make a life in the City of Halifax. Now the city did allow us $500 for furniture. You cannot get too much for $500, and you were only allowed certain things, no luxuries ... well, you couldn't get luxuries out of that anyhow.

The squatters — I hear a lot of talk about squatters and squatters' rights and if anyone cares to look it up, they'll find it means that they don't pay taxes but they have certain rights — were given $500. The homeowners were given more — I don't know how much — but it wasn't enough to buy a home. They were given this and told, "You go on now into the city, or go wherever you want to go and this is it." The city

did allow one month's rent. After that, we were on our own.

When I first moved from Africville, Uniacke Square [a housing project in the north end of Halifax] was in the process of being built, so I moved down to Barrington Street and I stayed there for about two years before I moved to Uniacke Square.

Living in Africville, we had our own home. It might not have been a mansion, but it was a home. Then we turn around and come into a city and have to pay rent.

We went along with that, thinking we had to do all this. We were under the impression then that if they said move, you go, if they said come, you come. It would never happen today.

Another thing I often think about is our families. The majority of us had large families and today a lot of our families have gone to Montreal, Toronto, out West, the United States and all over. They say, "Well, Mom, there is nothing much to stay around here for,

Clarence Carvery.

down different things and I began to think, Laura, what is happening to you? Where are these things coming from? And I began to think about the spirit of Africville, and to me it is so beautiful and so precious.

One day things are going to be right. I may not live to see it, but some of my children, or my children's children are going to see a different world than we are living in today.

Irvine Carvery's older brother, Clarence, who now lives in Halifax on a disability pension, was another of the youngsters whose lives were disrupted by the bulldozers.

CLARENCE CARVERY: It is such an enjoyable time remembering all of the little children's games we used to play. I can look at some people here and I can say, "I remember you, so don't say nothing to me, if you say something to me I will squeal on you."

I can remember as a young boy, one day I swore and Mrs. Ruth Johnson — a great leader — was coming out of our house. She said, "Dickie, is that you?" I said, "Yes." She said, "I don't want to hear that coming out of your mouth again." Well, neither did she, because I knew what was coming.

The community itself meant so much. Playing, swimming ... to wake up in the morning and run down and jump right off the rock in the water, tide in or out. (laughter)

We used to have picnics. I remember one year we had a church picnic and we had it down in Kildare's Field, but we had it down in a little gully. I remember Stan Carvery, my uncle, built these straw huts — you would swear to God you were in Hawaii. (laughter) — and after they got it built, an awful windstorm came up and blew it all down. We still had the picnic though, and the water came right up from the Basin and flooded the field. The next time they built it, they built it up on the higher ground.

I look at the panel, I remember Mrs. Howe's son, Kenney. He and I used to hang around. I remember Grandmother leaning over the table saying, "What are you doing? Why are they taking my home?" I said, "Grandmother, I don't know."

I can remember trucks coming in. I remember Mrs. Sarah Mantley's house — they tore it down, they never gave her time to take a stitch of furniture out of her home and knocked it down. They bulldozed it.

I will have to go away so I can make a better living," which they all did. That too hurt. You have to leave your home and go away to make a living for yourself.

We began to wonder, why is this being done to us? Everything just seemed to be against us, but one thing we always kept in mind was the faith. We kept the faith that one day things are going to turn around. When I look around now I see so many things. I look at my television and I look at that Berlin Wall and I saw how that came down. I began to think of scripture — the walls of Jericho — and then I said, there is nothing impossible. And I thought, if the day ever comes that South Africa will be free, I don't think we'll be able to contain it.

I thought about it in bed last night and so many things came to me, I had to get up at 4 o'clock this morning and I began to write it, and I began to jot

Mr. James Stewart was in Camp Hill Hospital and they bulldozed the house down, the man didn't even know. He came out of the hospital and had no place to go. These are the things I remember. I don't forget them.

Like Mrs. Howe stated, I remember the church going down. I was one of the young fellows out early that morning. I remember the city truck going there. I was saying, "You can't tear the church down, the people aren't gone yet."

I am very pleased to have this chance to talk about these things today because if everybody listens they can see how bad we were hurt, and how much we are still being hurt.

When the city rushed us out and tore it down, they tore our hearts away. But we are still surviving right to this very day, and we will survive and we will go on forever.

Terry Dixon, who now works for Maritime Telephone and Telegraph Company in Halifax, was 12 when his family was moved.

TERRY DIXON: When I came here I had no idea the amount of emotion that this was going to bring up in me. I share some of the memories of Africville that have been talked about and I have some of my own. I was twelve when we left so at that time it was just exciting. I didn't understand exactly what it was all about. Now, as I look back, there are two points I'd just like to make.

Terry Dixon.

One of them is about living conditions. That was one of the things that they used against us, the city saying that our living conditions were substandard. What I would like to say is that maybe they weren't up to the standard of the people who set the standards, but these were our homes, no matter what the houses looked like.

Africville was not alone. There were other communities, and not just black communities, where living conditions were not the best. Terence Bay and a lot of other communities had the same type of living conditions, if not worse. But we were close to the city and we were predominantly black. So our living conditions were used as a reason to move us — even though our situation could have easily been upgraded with some plumbing, some paved roads the city would not give us.

There is an evolutionary process that takes place in a black community. This can be seen in any community in Nova Scotia, but I'd like to use North Preston, East Preston and Cherry Brook as an example. Twenty years ago, if you drove through those communities, you would see houses that reminded you of Africville; Some of them were just foundations with a roof, some of them were bigger homes with an outhouse in the back, others were just little shacks. Today, if you drive through those communities, you will see some homes that should be in a magazine. They were built with hard work and perseverance, but we in Africville were not given the opportunity to be a part of that evolutionary process.

The people of my generation especially will feel the effects of the relocation forever. Imagine for a moment that you were a young person living in Africville with your parents. You were given a small piece of land by your father or your grandparents. You built your home

Above: Uniacke Square, site of relocation for some Africville residents.
Left: Youth at an Africville reunion, held once a year.

on that piece of land. You paid cash for everything. It took you two years or more of hard work and you put every penny and every free moment into building this home. After two years, you had a home, a piece of land, mortgage free. It gave you an opportunity to bring up your own family and have a good start. You had financial security.

My generation has been deprived of this opportunity. We will struggle for everything we get, because somebody decided that the land of Africville would serve the city better as industrial land. They should think again.

The second point I would like to talk about is Africville the community. When you read an article about Africville you are sure to find the phrase, "sense of loss." Although it may seem like an overused phrase, it really describes what we feel.

Some of us were relocated to Uniacke Square in the downtown area and we adapted to that community,

Linda Mantley.

but something was missing because we didn't grow up there. We adapted, we accepted, but it just wasn't ours. Some of us have homes in Sackville now, and in Dartmouth, and they're homes that we might own. They're nice communities and we get along with our neighbours, but something is missing.

Then once a year, we venture out to Africville for our reunion. We set up our tents, we set up our campers or throw a blanket on the grass. The children are playing, people are laughing and hugging and reminiscing about the old days. For three days, we have our community back. We stop for just one moment, we look at the train tracks, we smell the salt water air, we hear the sound of the waves in the Basin, all those sounds that bring back everything that we felt and we say, now this is mine.

Linda Mantley, one of the founders of the Africville Genealogy Society, now works for the Social Planning Department, City of Halifax.

LINDA MANTLEY: I am very emotional today. It seems that we have lost more than our homes. Being young and living there, I remember I had to be in church at least three times on Sunday because my father was a deacon. I remember playing ball, swimming. I think I got scared when I fell off a log one time and I would not swim anymore. But it was just all that freedom, picking berries, just being free — freedom that you never have again.

I guess I speak for my friend Deborah [Dixon-Jones] today. Without her the Africville Genealogy Society would not be here. It was a dream that she had. Deborah wanted to bring back the unity we shared in the Africville community, the concern that was shown when trouble or disaster came to the community, the togetherness.

But it became harder after the relocation. Why did someone have to die or marry to bring us together? When did we get together, how often did we talk

View from the field looking up to Big Town.

about Africville with one another and have a good laugh about some of the things, or even fill up because we missed it? So many memories, even the sad ones, became cherished because they had a part of Africville. That's the reason for the society and why we have our three-day reunion each year. There are people that live in the United States, up through Canada, who cherish those three days every year.

Listen to the words of Debbie Dixon. "Africville was my home and when people ask where I am from, I say with pride, Africville. For it was my parents and all of you who gave me love, helped me along in life's path as a youngster, who shared whatever they had, who built understanding, so we can one day find that."

In closing, I just hope that I can read this beautiful poem, "Africville My Home." It was written by Terry Dixon.

Another time, another place,
But the memories are vivid and strong.
From Big Town
to Round the Turn,
We had a place to belong.

Remember the closeness of neighbors and friends.
Our elders so greatly respected.
And in our own small world, of that freedom and love,
Our unity kept us protected.

City living was fine for others,
But our haven out home reigned above.
Very true it is that we had our faults,
But our foundation was built on love.
In days gone by, our village stood strong,
City politics led us astray.
Let others learn from our misjudgments,
Trust never what they say.

Let the young ones learn what once was,
With pictures and tales of the land.
Each of us must teach them this,
Don't let go of what's yours, take a stand.

My homeland they've taken, my culture they've blemished,
We no longer live together.
Yet ever so hard as they may try,
Africville will live forever.

Hold us close, Jesus, my friend,
Help us to re-unite
Over each and every obstacle.
Be our heart, our strength, our sight.

Many years have passed us by,
But remember that shoreline view.
Enable us to reach back once more,
Re-unite us in one on you.

Ruth Johnson, who contributed a great many artifacts to the exhibition, is the matriarch of a founding Africville family.

RUTH JOHNSON: This is an honour for me to be here today. My great-grandfather was the first settler in Africville. John Brown, his wife, Tom Brown, unmarried, and William Brown, just the three of them with some tools. They were the ones who were placed here from Africa. Africville was nothing but bush. Maybe [the white authorities] thought they were going to Bedford Basin to drown themselves, but they didn't.

I was born in a house with plastered walls and a dining room and a living room and a butler's pantry and parlour that we were not allowed to go in, but the best of furniture. Anybody can come to my house now to see some of the beautiful furniture that came from Africville — linen tablecloths, out of this world silver, beautiful things. There were lots of lovely homes.

There was not a home in Africville that didn't have a piano or an organ. This is why we used to go around after church and learn how to sing. We didn't need anybody to teach us how to give music. All my sisters, all of us went to the Conservatory of Music and took music, from the violin right down to the pipe organ, and taught it to the children.

So we were somebodies, we had our own stores, we

Ruth Johnson.

had our church, our schools, we had our teachers, we had our own ministers who were born in Africville. One of the world's greatest boxers that you know was black, George Dixon was born right in Africville. Duke Ellington's wife, her father came right from Africville, so there were some very good people who came from Africville.

But Africville people were people who didn't blow their own trumpets. Unless you looked down over the hill, maybe you thought they were in Bedford Basin. But they were still down there living, minding their own business because they didn't need anybody else, they didn't need to go to anybody. They made their living, they worked at different companies and they worked and paid their taxes. They cannot say that the people in Africville were squatters because the ones who paid taxes paid a whole lot of taxes for those who were squatters. Any "squatters" were squatting on Brown

Brenda Steed-Ross.

land. When the city imposed taxes on the Browns, the Browns paid their taxes. I can show you taxes when it was $19.20 a year right up to $385 in 1967 when they brought Africville out.

But you know, education is a must. If you don't know the big words and you don't look at the fine print ... this is how we were cheated. The City was very dirty and they got the uneducated ones to say, "Oh, a couple hundred dollars is good for you. You can take that and live in the city." But my father fished in the Basin and got all our codfish and salted it down. We had dories and everything. There was a slaughterhouse where we could get all our meats. The boys worked at the slaughterhouse and could get all the free meats.

What did the City ever give us in Africville? My grandmother, Mrs. Jessie MacDonald, had to petition for every darn thing they got in Africville. There were no street lights, she had to petition the City for that.

The City is no good. Maybe some of them will rot in hell for some of the dirty deeds they did to the Blacks.

(applause) Let me tell the City this, because the City has been just cheating the black people too long in life just because they are white. Thank you. (applause)

Brenda Steed-Ross's father, Leon, was one of the key spokespeople for Africville residents during the relocation. His daughter became one of the organizers of the Africville Genealogy Society and served as its president. Now a bookkeeper in Halifax, she chaired this panel discussion.

BRENDA STEED-ROSS: Thank you very much, Aunt Ruth. I am very glad you were able to come this morning. We have had comments from all of our panelists and their feelings are the same as mine.

We think of all the memories we have of our home, how much it meant to us as young people and also the move, how we didn't realize then what was going on. We were moving. But as the years go on and we start thinking back and we are missing this freedom that we have talked about today. We are missing the closeness, our elders, our church, the important part that it was in our community. The church was our backbone.

Our elders, they were the church and that's where we got our guidance and the talking to when we were doing things that were a little bit off, but they would set us straight and try to give us a guideline. Their words were guidelines that followed us through life, things that we can think back on. We do not forget those and I really do salute my elders.

I would also like to thank everybody for being here today.

At the conclusion of the session, Irvine Carvery invited comments and questions from the audience.

"I just want to make one brief remark," offered Halifax filmmaker Bill McKeigan quietly. "We often talk about community or try to figure out why there is no community in Halifax. I would really like to thank the panelists because they have told me what real community is in this city."

Reverend Charles Coleman agreed. Coleman, who had been minister of Africville's Seaview Baptist Church during much of the relocation period and served as an Africville representative on the committee that had advised the City on relocation issues, had returned to Halifax to take part in the conference.

REVEREND CHARLES COLEMAN: I will make two comments. One is that as I listen to you talk today, the depths of emotion and the impact it had on you — a group that was not really considered in our consultation, we did not ask the young people any-thing — reminds me of part of the Bible where it says, how can I sing the songs of Zion where they're in a strange nation. I was moved, almost like crying, and I understand where you are coming from and I just want to encourage you to stay with it.

The other comment I want to make is that I think there is a lot of good will still circulating in Halifax, Nova Scotia. Take advantage of the good will that is here, but you have to have the realization — I realize now more since I have come and listened to you — that you have a sense of power, a feeling that you can do something.

A lot of us on that committee got to a point that we had a sense of powerlessness. We did the best that we could and it still would seem like new forces are coming up.

Why did moving families and destroying a community seem like the best that could be done? When Clarence and Irvine Carvery's grandmother, Hattie, asked them 25 years ago why she had to move, neither of them could come up with an answer that made any sense to them. Neither could Laura Howe.

They still can't.

That is one reason why conference organizers made a point of inviting some of the key players in the Africville relocation, including Reverend Coleman, to talk about — and reflect upon — the crucial decisions they made so long ago.

Toronto-based community organizer Alan Borovoy wasn't an Africville decision-maker himself, but he did serve as a kind of catalyst who helped organize a critically important citizen's committee — made up of both Africville and non-Africville residents — that negotiated with the City on behalf of the community. Today Borovoy is the long-time General Counsel of the Canadian Civil Liberties Association.

ALAN BOROVOY: I hope you will appreciate that I was here involved in the Africville situation in the year 1962, and I spent a little over four days here.

I think there are two key inferences that have to be drawn from the Africville experience. One is an easy

Alan Borovoy.

one and the other is a more difficult one.

The easy one is that Africville people got less than they believed they were entitled to because they lacked the clout to do better. In the real world, it is not reason that produces results, it's pressure. Unless you are will-ing and able to raise hell, you don't get. I don't want anyone to get the impression that I'm opposed to reason. Pressure without reason is irresponsible, but reason without pressure is ineffectual.

The second, much more difficult inference is that organizations composed of economically disadvantaged people don't spring full blown out of the stratosphere. It takes hard, gruelling, drudging work. Volunteers are not likely to be able to do it, part-timers are not likely to be able to do it. It very often requires a full-time staff whose primary loyalty is to the organization. That means it requires money.

The Africville people didn't have the money, so some-body had to come along and provide money for staff in order to build the kind of organization that would have enabled them to exert the clout they needed to exert on their own behalf. Money is the prerequisite for self-determination.

I read in the Clairmont and Magill book that there was a contrast between the approach I used when I was here in 1962 and that used by the legendary American radical, Saul Alinsky. When I was here, I helped to organ-ize the Halifax Human Rights Advisory Committee, an alliance of Africville and non-Africville people. The book points out that Alinsky always believed you must create an indigenous people's organization before you

Gus Wedderburn.

create alliances with others.

I want to assure you that the differences between Alinsky and me on this score were not strategic. They were financial. Alinsky went into those communities with hundreds of thousands of dollars, full-time staff, and he stayed for a few years. I was here in Halifax alone, and I was here for four days, and I wasn't sure I could get the plane fare to get home. It makes a difference.

All I suggest is that if we are serious about helping to build people's organizations so that they can have a real say, and that means clout, then we have to look at the tough question of where the seed money is going to come from.

Unless we consider this question, tomorrow's Africvilles will be no less screwed than yesterday's.

One of those who became an important member of the Halifax Human Rights Advisory Committee that Borovoy organized was a young school teacher named Gus Wedderburn. Wedderburn, a Caribbean native, had moved to Halifax just a few years before the relocation began. He is now a Halifax lawyer.

GUS WEDDERBURN: When I first arrived in Halifax in 1957, I walked along Barrington Street off Spring Garden Road, and I looked in the windows of the office, banks, the stores and on the streets. I saw no coloured people.

So I said to my friends, "Where are the coloured people of Halifax?" And they said to me, "They live in a place called Africville." I asked, "Would someone take me to Africville?" My friends drove me along Barrington Street. Where the pavement ended, Africville began.

I did not see the flowers.

As we drove through Africville, I could see the concrete pipes, which they explained to me were the sewer pipes that led material from Halifax City into the harbour.

I did not see the flowers.

Where Africville ended, the city dump began. As we drove through the dump I saw my brothers scavenging on the dump.

I did not see the flowers.

I heard stories about Africville. I heard the story of a dog barking in Africville, and the barking annoyed a white lady who lived on a hill overlooking Africville. She called the police and a policeman was dispatched. He went into the home where that dog was barking and shot the dog.

It was sometime around Christmas when we picked up a newspaper. In it was the story of a family in Africville that had been burning old car batteries which had been scavenged on the dump to keep them warm and, as a result of burning those batteries, the family was lead poisoned and had to be taken to the hospital.

I asked myself the question, God, what is this? What is this?

At the time, the civil rights movement was getting going in the United States, and Martin Luther King was talking about the brotherhood of man and of each of us being our brothers' keepers. I felt it incumbent upon me to do something to help my brothers. As a result, when I was invited to attend a meeting dealing with Africville and the decision of the city fathers of Halifax to remove the residents from Africville, I figured I had to be there.

Alan Borovoy spoke with the group, and we organized the Halifax Human Rights Advisory Committee, with a mandate to do what we could to assist the residents of Africville. We met many times with the City of Halifax and urged them to move slowly and cautiously because they were dealing with people's lives. There were several meetings in Africville. In the church itself, a committee was struck which involved members of the community of Africville. This committee was given the mandate to represent the citizens of Africville. I had the honour of being asked to act as its chairman.

As a consequence of our meetings with the people of Africville and with the City Council, Dr. Albert Rose was brought in as a consultant to write a report dealing with the relocation. A full-time social worker was employed with the specific responsibility to assist the individual citizens and their move. Each move that was made was presented to a giant committee of our advisory committee and representatives of the City Council of Halifax.

I maintain that at the time we did what we did because we considered it to be in the best interests of everyone. It was our understanding that Africville was going to go. It was our understanding that this was a part of the implementation of the Stephenson Report, which had to do with the future development of the Halifax waterfront.

Several decades later I look back as others have done, and ask myself a question. Would I have acted today as I did then? Of course the response is no.

In conclusion, I believe that the community and the lands of Africville should be returned to the former residents or the descendants of Africville. I believe that a model community could be built, that homes could be built, and the descendants of the residents of Africville could be invited to return because I would like to see the flowers.

One of Africville's most influential representatives during the relocation process was Charles Coleman, the pastor of the Seaview Baptist Church. Coleman, an American, was deeply involved with the Africville relocation during the negotiations with the City but returned to the US before the relocation itself was completed.

REVEREND CHARLES COLEMAN: I had questions about coming here today, about calling myself a decision maker. The decision makers refer to the City Council, the mayor and other employees of the City. Does it include the Halifax Human Rights Commission? Does it include Africville residents appointed and designated as the leaders of Africville? I think the decision-makers included all of the above, plus the newspaper and other behind-the-scenes power brokers.

The residents of Africville did not have the power or financial resources or the people power to do what they

Reverend Charles Coleman.

wanted to do — that is, to remain on their land and get the government to finance a resurrection of a crucified people, who had been crucified by years of neglect.

The neglected, the system-enslaved people, took the best way out — at least they thought it was the best way out and, really, it was a no-win situation. A person or people must be judged and must be understood in the light of the historical situation.

Those people who suffered to help us in Africville sought to help us because they were our friends. The Whites who were involved on the committee were there because they felt that those in Africville were their sisters and their brothers of a different colour. They gave of their money, and they gave of their time, they gave of all the resources they had to help us make some decisions for the benefit of the people in Africville.

Those who live today do not know the agony that we went through. We made decisions because we could not put off decisions any longer. We did what we had to because it seemed to be the best alternative for the choices before us.

Allan O'Brien, who later served as Mayor of Halifax, was one of the fourteen City Councillors faced with deciding Africville's fate in the early 1960s. He is now a consultant on urban issues.

ALLAN O'BRIEN: I was certainly one of the decision makers. I come to you tonight to speak to this because I think we ought to be open about it. I come not to speak in either pride or apology, but to try to

Allan O'Brien.

speak about how we — the members of City Council — saw it when we made the decision.

What I have to say is not, I expect, what some of you would like to hear.

For the record, let me say I do not believe that that momentous decision that we made in 1964 would be made now the way it was made then. And if it were made in a way which would be acceptable now, it would not have been made at all. What decision might have been made, I do not know. But that is all hind-sight, which, as you know, is 20/20.

What was it that we did as decision makers? First, we accepted the advice of City staff, the advice of an out-side expert, Albert Rose, and the advice of the Halifax Human Rights Advisory Committee. Second, we, the members of Council, chose relocation over all other alternatives.

Why did we chose relocation? I think I heard on the radio within the last week that one of the reasons was to make way for the container pier that is in Fairview Cove. Well, that is not on Africville lands and it was not even thought about then.

I have heard it said frequently that it had to do with making way for the bridge. Well, at the time that we made that decision, Halifax City Council was fight-ing very hard to have that bridge put in the south end of the city. When we made our decision, we had no intention of seeing any bridge anywhere near there. The Magill-Clairmont report says that the reason was because of a proposal for an industrial mile along the shores of Bedford Basin at the north end of the city, a strip that would take in Africville and a good deal of additional lands. Now I know that this was in some planning proposals which were approved in principle by City Council, but I want to tell you that planning proposals that get approved like that often are only plans on paper. By the time in 1964 that we came to make this decision, the argument about industrial lands was nowhere to be heard.

Some suggest maybe we were doing it for a site for expensive residential development. Well that did not happen and I know of no such proposals.

Well, what were the reasons? As Gus has said, that was a time when the currents in the wind of public opinion had to do with questions of housing conditions, integra-tion or desegregation, and we felt on the Council that a lot needed to be done in Halifax. When we moved to go ahead with the Scotia Square development [a shop-ping centre/office/hotel/apartment complex in what had been a low-income central Halifax neighbourhood], we acquired all the properties there and forced people to go elsewhere. We offered them public housing. Quite a few went to Mulgrave Park.

Africville came after that and, in the pattern of those City policies, we decided that something different needed to be done in Africville and that is why we hired a social worker to do the negotiating, why the compen-sation was based on need rather than having clear title to the land and what the property value was. Maybe that does not sound right today and I agree that there is a lot about this that does not sound right today.

We were also persuaded that the public services could be supplied more easily if we moved the people elsewhere. That's another one which even I would question today but I did not question it then and I don't know others who seriously questioned that in the decision-making process, including all our advisors and Council itself.

We also wanted to promote integration and get rid of ghettos. We believed we could achieve that better by moving people to public housing and other kinds of housing that might be available.

And there was another final reason for the reloca-tion. No one should be proud of it particularly, but I think that the total Halifax community was somewhat embarrassed by the degree of publicity about having a so-called "slum" as part of the city. As a result, some action was pushed on us by that particular feeling. That action was the relocation of the residents of Africville.

Frankly, I don't think we on the Council had a lot

of information about the fairly lengthy history of Africville. I've learned a lot about the historical part of Africville from reading the Clairmont-Magill study, but I don't recall being informed about that at the time that we were making the decision. When you read a lot of that in detail, it makes an impression on you that you don't get from a few sentences said or written at a time when you're looking at what is one item out of fifty on a City Council agenda.

Looked at from today, I have to say that I think we also undervalued the importance of a sense of community.

If I were a member of City Council today and this proposition came before us, I think I would say — and I think probably every member of the Council would say today — that the Council had better go down there and hold public hearings in the church and listen to the residents directly.

But following the practices of the time, we listened to people we had a great respect for — both white and black members of the Human Rights Advisory Committee — who reported to us that Africville residents had accepted the Rose report because of a vote which occurred in a meeting in the church where only 41 were present, but 37 voted to accept the report. The Human Rights Advisory Committee told us that they were unanimously approving the Rose report, and I think the motives of all the people were the best.

Now when you come to City Council members and the City Hall staff, people do have other agendas, whether bureaucrats or politicians and I can't speak for all of the persons involved. But I do know that we had some very conscientious City staff who wanted to do the right thing, but the right thing and the implementation side may not always have been done and I think it wasn't always done.

Despite the best efforts of O'Brien and the other panelists, many in the audience found their answers less than satisfactory.

Carrie Toussaint, for example, a descendant of Africville residents, said she had hoped to hear "some answers to a question that I've been asking my family for a long time."

"Why did they do that to people?" asked Toussaint. "I've heard a lot of statements from you gentlemen about integration and desegregation, things like that, and I really still don't understand. Did you use Africville for a test — were the people guinea pigs for something new?

That is my question. Because I still, sitting here listening to you, do not understand exactly what took place."

Others, including Halifax social activist Jackie Barkley, believed they understood only too well. "I guess what I'm concerned about," Barkley said at the conclusion of the formal presentations, "is that we've been here for almost an hour-and-a-half now and the one phrase that hasn't been articulated is the one about racism. We face a situation where Africvilles exist in the present. If we don't learn from the history of Africville that there is racism now, we're really wasting our time. The lessons of then have to be understood in the present and we, particularly those of us who are white in this audience and in this community, have a responsibility to understand the fact that the oppression that occurred 25 years ago exists in the present and we have a responsibility to fight it now."

What about this reality of what Barkley — and others at the conference — referred to as the Africvilles that exist in the present? The final segment of the conference focused on what should be done to make sure that those communities do not suffer the same fate as Africville but also on what to do to respond to the legitimate grievances of the residents of Africville and their descendants.

Dr. Fred MacKinnon, who was Nova Scotia's deputy minister of welfare at the time of the Africville relocation and now — in retirement — serves as an advisor to the provincial senior citizen's secretariat, offered the conference a no-nonsense assessment of what can be learned from the mistakes that were made in Africville.

DR. FRED MACKINNON: The central question is this: How does one improve the social and economic conditions of a whole community where unemployment is rampant and far above the national average, where education is being neglected by the educational authorities, where housing has to be improved and where the services of sewer, light, water, recreation and the like are lacking?

That challenge faced the decision-makers in respect to Africville in 1964, and there are still black and white communities in Nova Scotia today where the social and economic hardships faced by the community are not greatly different from those that faced Africville — except in degree. That is why it is important that we learn some lessons from the mistakes that we made in the past.

I think we have to learn that many such communities, and Africville is a prime example, have a cultural

Fred MacKinnon.

identity, a personality and an emotional place in the hearts and minds of their people which could provide the solid foundation for the future growth and development of that community.

I think the first fundamental lesson to be learned about such communities is that social and economic change cannot be manipulated, and I underline the word manipulated. We used to believe in the manipulation of people and, unfortunately, some still do. We thought that we could manipulate change in our Native people, for example, and so we sent them to Indian schools to make them over in the white image and culture. They lost their own culture and didn't take ours.

I was a party personally in those early years to the manipulation of children, believing that if they were removed from their own homes and placed in foster homes they would do better there. Perhaps some of them do. But the failure rate was far, far too high, and many of them would have been better off if their families had been given adequate support and help and if they were left and helped there. I could go on and on with examples like that.

Africville was a victim of the belief that somehow we

could manipulate the culture, the traditions and the sense of community of a people, but it doesn't work. It hasn't worked and it won't work.

Social and economic change for me personally, or for a community, has to begin not where you or someone else thinks that I should be, not there, but where I am. Now you may not like where I am, and you may not like what I'm doing, but if you're going to effect social and economic change with me or with a community, you have to begin where I am, where that community is.

It's a long, slow process, and unfortunately the media is very impatient, and always looks for the quick and easy fix. And the media simply reflects people. We're all prone to think that the mistakes of a hundred years can be remedied in a hurry, and they cannot.

The second lesson to be learned relates to the manner in which the relocation was carried out. Let us assume that the option of relocation was the preferred and best option. The relocation could only have succeeded if there was persistent follow-up and support for at least a decade after the move. How can you uproot people, transplant them and expect them to succeed in a new and strange environment without support? We didn't provide that support, and that alone spelled disaster.

[Premier Joseph] Smallwood made precisely the same error in Newfoundland, when he moved people from the outports into the more settled parts of Newfoundland, left them there and didn't follow-up what had been started.

The lesson to be learned then is: don't trust long-term commitments, in government or otherwise, unless, as Alan Borovoy said, you have money and power and clout to force the government and others to listen to you, and not forget that you exist.

Social and economic justice is an elusive goal for which we all strive. We can draw some satisfaction from the fact that we have learned from the mistakes of yesterday, and some of them we will not repeat tomorrow. That's good. My personal concern is that, having surveyed the past, as we are doing here, we shall have the will, the courage and the wisdom to apply what we have learned to other communities in Nova Scotia that need to be helped as well. These are communities where unemployment is far too high, where the educational, cultural and recreational resources need to be improved greatly and where housing had been neglected.

Surely some good shall come from all of this, if we have learned the lessons that we should have learned and get at the task of helping these other communities to help themselves.

Reverend Donald Skeir, who is the pastor of the black communities in Preston, North Preston and Cherrybrook, says the larger black community in Nova Scotia has already learned well the lessons of Africville.

REVEREND DONALD SKEIR: The people in power were not concerned by what happened to the black people in Africville. They always had that self-styled God complex, that we could not think, that we could not make decisions, that they must do all our decision-making for us.

Everybody went through the exercise of having meetings with the people there but, behind it all, decisions had already been made. That was prime land. That was important land. There were those, and I'm sure that there were those in the Preston area too when we were moved out further and further, who believed this kind of land was not for the black people.

I suggest to you that for many, many generations the power authorities in the city knew the horrible conditions that existed in Africville. There was need for better sanitary conditions, there was need for housing, there was need for education and so forth. They overlooked a fact that black people are human beings, that we can think and that we can feel, and there's no place like home, no matter what the conditions might be.

A few years ago when we went through similar confrontations between the City of Dartmouth and North Preston, the thought uppermost was "Remember Africville." We as black people cannot exist as ourselves whether in the community or in the province. We have to be unified. We have to realize that the only thing that people are going to listen to is the people themselves.

Social workers may be very sincere, government officials may be very interested in meeting a situation, but there's nothing better than hearing from the people themselves. We did not do that in 1964. Now we are looking back. Now we are trying to correct our thinking in regard to how we thought then. It can be a valuable experience. It can be a lesson that we learn.

Africville could still be a community on Bedford Basin. It could still be a housing development on Bedford Basin. There could now be a paved highway through the community of Africville on Bedford Basin. There could be a transit system through the community

Reverend Donald Skeir.

of Africville. Yes, all these things that we see developing in other parts of our area could have been in Africville, but God knows it will never, never, never happen again.

For Reverend Skeir and for many in both the black and white communities in Nova Scotia, Africville has now become more symbol than community — a tragedy not to be repeated.

Allister Johnson, President of the North Preston Ratepayers' Association, offered concrete evidence of just how well other black communities in Nova Scotia have learned the lessons of Africville.

ALLISTER JOHNSON: I remember as a teenager in 1977 or 1978, when our watershed issue came up, we learned that at the same time that the City of Halifax was planning the death of Africville, the City of Dartmouth was planning, in collaboration with the County of Halifax and behind the back of the local County Councillor, the death of North Preston.

Fortunately, because of what happened in Africville, we learned. We knew that the key thing to do was not only to be organized but to be our own organizers and our own leaders.

In 1989, as Reverend Skier just mentioned, we have also proven that what the City of Halifax said about not being able to provide water and sewer to Africville because of the rocky ground was a myth. I doubt if there is any harder rock — outside Newfoundland — than the rock North Preston sits on, but we got water and sewer. It could have been done in Africville too.

I remember talking to Brother Carvery in North Preston some years ago and he indicated to me

Allister Johnson.

— and this really struck home — that once he was an heir to a piece of property. Now, the descendants of Africville are tenants.

There was so much potential, but it was all robbed from the residents of Africville.

The City of Halifax owes the people of Africville. The City should seriously look at providing Africville with property so that the people of Africville can begin to develop themselves as a community — not just spiritually as they are now, but physically as well.

I would like to be able to get in my car one day and drive through Africville.

So would Irvine Carvery. He still considers Africville home — he doesn't want to be referred to as a former resident of the community, but as a resident.

For Irvine Carvery and his fellow members of the Africville Genealogy Society, in fact, there is still unfinished business that needs to be taken care of. As he explained it at the conference:

IRVINE CARVERY: Last year, just a little over a year ago, the Africville Genealogy Society petitioned the City for certain things and certain actions that we would like to see take place in regard to the land that's still out in Africville. One of our demands was for the City of Halifax to consider relocating the people back to the land of Africville. The land is underutilized, it's idle land and the people want to go back to the land, so why not move back?

We would like to propose to the Province of Nova Scotia and the Government of Canada and the City of Halifax that we institute a guaranteed sale of homes for the people of Africville who now own their own homes, guarantee us sale of their homes at appraised value if we relocate back to our land.

As you know, there are lots of people from Africville who do not own their own homes. The cooperative housing movement in the City of Halifax has just mushroomed over the last five years. That is another kind of housing that can be provided for the people of Africville.

Then, of course, you have your public housing. That also can be instituted into a planned community that is participated in by and with the people of Africville.

There are the ways and means, there is the initiative, there is the will and the power of the people of Africville to move back to their land. All we need is the involvement and the commitment of our government officials. We will be continuing that push.

What I would ask from the people who have attended the exhibit in the art gallery or the sessions here this weekend is that you support us, the people of Africville, in our efforts to get back to where we came from.

The conference ended with the impromptu singing of a song Ruth Johnson had written about Africville. As Johnson lead the singing, white and black voices joined in harmony on the chorus.

Oh, Africville, Africville
No more can I call you my home
Oh Africville, Africville
I want to go home.

Whether the Africville residents and their descendants will ever get to "go home" is far from resolved, but Irvine Carvery says that the Africville exhibition and conference made him and other members of the Genealogy Society realize that they are not alone in their struggle. "We discovered that there are a lot of people out there who support us and we also discovered that the issue is bigger than just Africville."

CHAPTER 5

BEFORE AFRICVILLE:
NOVA SCOTIA'S BLACK SETTLERS

BRIDGLAL PACHAI

When the last house in the Africville settlement was demolished on January 6, 1970 a chapter closed in the lives of some 80 black families — about 400 individuals. With the closing down of the settlement, it could be argued that what happened here, why it happened, and when it happened, stand without comparison with any other black settlement in the history of Nova Scotia. But for all its uniqueness, and for all the special lessons derived from it, the experience of Africville is an integral part of the black experience in Nova Scotia. The account of the Africville community over its 120-year history speaks for the many other black settlements throughout Nova Scotia which were established at different times throughout the eighteenth and nineteenth centuries. What happened during these centuries in the lives of the black people of Nova Scotia is integral to what happened in Africville and to the Africville residents.

This chapter reviews the conditions that gave rise to black settlements in Nova Scotia and describes the different immigration groups. It recounts the institutions and the personalities, as well as the occupations of the residents, the successes and the failures of their history and the legacies inherited and in turn passed on to succeeding generations.

INDIVIDUAL BLACK IMMIGRANTS

The first recorded Blacks in Nova Scotia were a scattered number of individuals who were attached to households as slaves or paid servants, or they were individual fortune seekers, perhaps even runaway slaves. Before the last quarter of the eighteenth century, when the Loyalist exodus from the United States brought some 30,000 new immigrants to Nova Scotia and New Brunswick, numbers were very small and black settlements as such were non-existent.

As early as 1605–1606, a black seaman, Mathieu da Costa, was

Above: A black woodcutter working in Shelburne, Nova Scotia, 1788.

associated with the seafarers at Port Royal, working for a fur-trading company. He is recorded as an interpreter of the French and Micmac languages at a time when the Acadians began trading with the Micmac people along the Atlantic coast of Nova Scotia. Though da Costa is believed to have died during the winter of 1606–1607, his place in the history of Blacks in Nova Scotia is assured because of his unique status when many of his fellow Africans were being sold as slaves.

The next record of black colonists shows the name "La Liberte, le neigre [*sic*]," a freed slave, who was listed as a resident of Cape Sable in 1686. After the founding of Halifax in 1749, the number of Blacks began to increase. In 1750, fifteen Blacks are reported to have obtained provisions in Halifax. The following year, ten Blacks from Halifax were put up for sale in Boston and advertised as tradesmen able to function as caulkers, carpenters, sailmakers and rope makers. Although most immigration at this time was from the New England colonies to Nova Scotia, this sale is evidence of some movement in the other direction. Combining the above with twenty Blacks who were advertised for sale in Halifax, it seems that forty-five Blacks were associated with Halifax in one way or other prior to 1752. Fifteen years later, in 1767, the number rose to 104 out of a total Nova Scotia population of 13,374.

By contrast, the Scots numbered fifty-two.[6]

Most of the black population fell into the category of persons in permanent bondage, whether or not they were called slaves. Among the free settlers was Barbara Cuffy, a black woman, who was associated with the founding of the town of Liverpool in 1760. Like the adventurous Africville pioneers of the 1840s who acquired land and put down roots, Barbara Cuffy became a shareholder in the township lands out of which Liverpool grew.

Mathieu da Costa (a seafarer), La Liberte (a slave) and Barbara Cuffy (a landowner): these three personify the nature of the early black experience in what has become Nova Scotia. Their lives individually represent the influence and immediacy of the sea, the plight and pathos of being denied a human existence, and the land as provider and custodian of life and liberty.

Similarly, in later times, Africville was shaped by these three influences — the seashore of Bedford Basin, the bondage of poverty and the value of the residents' small land holdings.

THE BLACK LOYALISTS

The third quarter of the eighteenth century was a time of revolution in politics and society in North America and Europe, highlighted by the American War of

A black family on Hammonds Plains Road near Bedford Basin, c. 1835.

Independence and by the French Revolution, both of which affected the fortunes of black people in North America. These international events were directly responsible for the first two organized movements of Blacks into Nova Scotia — the Black Loyalists in 1782–1784 and the Maroons in 1796. These two groups were the founders of the first black settlements in Nova Scotia.

Other ethnic groups migrating to Nova Scotia at this time were, however, not necessarily as strongly identified with their place of settlement. Take the case of Scottish immigration commencing with those on the *Hector* in 1773, and continuing throughout the next eighty years. Over a period of time, the Scots settled in Pictou and Antigonish counties and in Cape Breton and built viable economies. They were not necessarily highly skilled or otherwise well-to-do immigrants. We are told the "majority had little to offer but their muscle," and that on arrival "many hundreds were deposited in isolated locations [where] forced to learn quickly they made a successful adaptation."[7]

Scottish immigration and black immigration to Nova Scotia took place during the same period and they shared some of the same initial problems and challenges. However, the one outstanding difference is that the Scots were free from social barriers, whereas Blacks were impeded and weighed down by racial discrimination and were never able to prosper.

Like their nineteenth-century refugee counterparts, the Black Loyalists came to Nova Scotia at the British government's invitation. This was done through proclamations of freedom from slavery and offers of British protection issued by Governor Dunmore of Virginia in 1775, British Commander in New York Sir William Howe in 1776, and British Commander-in-Chief Sir Henry Clinton in 1779. Over a period of four years, Blacks were exhorted to cross over from their American masters to their new British masters, to sign up to do battle as members of the Black Ethiopian Regiment or simply to await shipment to a part of the Empire where they would live as free persons under British protection.

It was only when the peace agreement was signed on November 30,1782 and the black immigrants were recorded in the Book of Negroes, certifying that they were indeed free to emigrate, that some 3,000 of them were shipped to Nova Scotia. Up to October 13, 1783, their destinations and numbers were as follows: Port Roseway (later renamed Shelburne), 1312; Annapolis

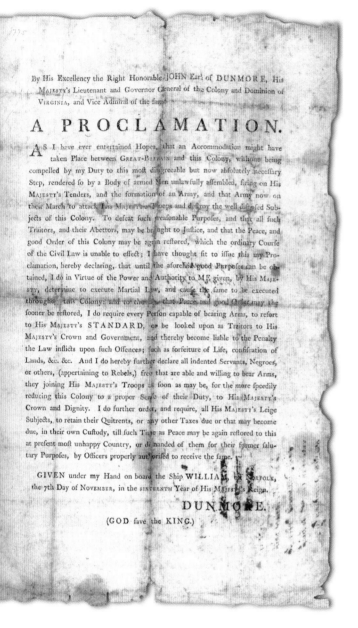

By His Excellency the Right Honorable JOHN Earl of DUNMORE, His Majesty's Lieutenant and Governor General of the Colony and Dominion of VIRGINIA, and Vice Admiral of the same

A PROCLAMATION.

AS I have ever entertained Hopes, that an Accommodation might have taken Place between GREAT-BRITAIN and this Colony, without being compelled by my Duty to this most disagreeable but now absolutely necessary Step, rendered so by a Body of armed Men unlawfully assembled, firing on His MAJESTY's Tenders, and the formation of an Army, and that Army now on their March to attack His Majesty's Troops and destroy the well disposed Subjects of this Colony. To defeat such treasonable Purposes, and that all such Traitors, and their Abettors, may be brought to Justice, and that the Peace, and good Order of this Colony may be again restored, which the ordinary Course of the Civil Law is unable to effect; I have thought fit to issue this my Proclamation, hereby declaring, that until the aforesaid good Purposes can be obtained, I do in Virtue of the Power and Authority to ME given, by His Majesty, determine to execute Martial Law, and cause the same to be executed throughout this Colony; and to the end that Peace and good Order may the sooner be restored, I do require every Person capable of bearing Arms, to resort to His MAJESTY's STANDARD, or be looked upon as Traitors to His MAJESTY's Crown and Government, and thereby become liable to the Penalty the Law inflicts upon such Offences; such as forfeiture of Life, confiscation of Lands, &c. &c. And I do hereby further declare all indented Servants, Negroes, or others, (appertaining to Rebels,) free that are able and willing to bear Arms, they joining His MAJESTY's Troops as soon as may be, for the more speedily reducing this Colony to a proper Sense of their Duty, to His MAJESTY's Crown and Dignity. I do further order, and require, all His MAJESTY's Liege Subjects, to retain their Quitrents, or any other Taxes due or that may become due, in their own Custody, till such Time as Peace may be again restored to this at present most unhappy Country, or demanded of them for their former salutary Purposes, by Officers properly authorised to receive the same.

GIVEN under my Hand on board the Ship WILLIAM, off NORFOLK, the 7th Day of NOVEMBER, in the SIXTEENTH Year of His Majesty's Reign.

DUNMORE.

(GOD save the KING.)

Proclamation from John Earl of Dunmore offering freedom to slaves who would join the royal forces.

Royal, 397; Halifax, 73; St. John River, 1578.[8]

From this time on, government authorities organized the settlement of black immigrants, using a framework that was handed down and reinforced through the centuries: Blacks were treated differently from Whites, were settled separately in segregated areas, and were provided for by special arrangements. The result was a pattern of unequal relationship between Whites and Blacks from the beginning, a relationship which could be likened to master-servant, patron-client, ruler-ruled, privileged-unprivileged. In the context of European domination of the rest of the world through economic and political exploitation associated with colonialism, it could be argued that what was experienced by black Nova Scotians was normal. What destroys this theory is the fact that black Nova Scotians, whether Loyalists, refugees or Maroons, were brought to Nova Scotia by invitation of the British government, with promises of British justice, British freedom and British protection.

When the colourful flotilla of 300 ships dropped anchor at Port Roseway on May 4, 1783, Nova Scotia was unprepared for this colossal influx which increased the town's population by at least three times. Half the available land was already distributed through lavish land grants to British and New England immigrants. Governor John Parr was given firm instructions on how the available land was to be distributed among the new immigrants. The underlying principle was that those who lost the greatest amount of property should be given the largest grants in compensation. Next came the militia who were treated according to rank with land grants ranging from 405 hectares to 40.5 hectares. Finally, the ordinary Loyalist immigrants (among whom the black immigrants were placed) were to receive 40.5 hectares for the head of family and half that amount for every individual member. A grant of twenty hectares was computed for each slave which, of course, was issued to the each of the owners of the 1,232 slaves.

Many writers, notably James Walker,[9] have drawn attention to the tragedy underlying land grants to black immigrants in the Loyalist period. Had the guidelines given to Governor John Parr been adhered to strictly, the history of Blacks in Nova Scotia would have been quite different. Not only would there not have been the emigration of 1,196 Black Loyalists to Sierra Leone in 1792, but the quality of the black settlements would have been strong enough to counteract the hardships of isolation and discrimination. The large segregated settlements created in the Loyalist period in Birchtown (Shelburne), Brindley Town (Digby), Tracadie (Guysborough) and Preston, with smaller outposts in various parts of the province,

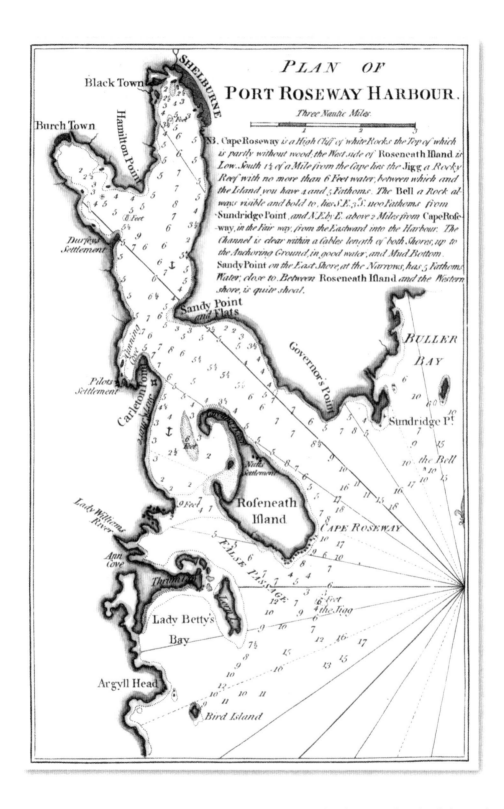

The town of Port Roseway was unprepared to have its population triple when 300 ships landed in its harbour on May 4, 1783.

went through a difficult period in the first decade of settlement, 1782–1792.

In the first six years, fewer than 500 Blacks, from a population of some 3,500, received any land grants at all. The average was less than one-third of that promised. The locality was usually a distant, desolate place. The quality was invariably barren, rocky, infertile and unsuitable for agriculture.

As the present author has stated elsewhere: "It was clear from the start that the Black Loyalist Nova Scotians were in for much trouble. The fact that all of them survived the first decade (1782–1792) and half of them became part of the permanent population of Nova Scotia is a tribute to their resilience and to their faith."[10]

Despite the tremendous odds faced by these pioneering black Nova Scotians between 1782 and 1792, their experience was invaluable in succeeding decades. First, the black presence became a Nova Scotian reality. Consider the distribution of settlements of black persons in various parts of Nova Scotia in the 1780s:

Birchtown 1521	Halifax 400
Brindley Town 211	Chedabucto (Canso) 350
Shelburne 200	Tracadie 222
Preston 300	Liverpool 50
Annapolis 100	

Second, collective leadership in the settlements was a beacon to guide future generations of activists. Every black community in Nova Scotia throughout the centuries has produced dedicated members who have served in various ways in religious and secular organizations. Figuratively speaking, the ships which navigated troubled and challenging waters stayed the course and weathered the storms because of the human resources which the community could draw from.

In the first period the names Mathieu da Costa, La Liberte and Barbara Cuffy stand out. The second period — the Loyalist period — produced its own list of notables, among them David George, the Baptist preacher from South Carolina, who arrived in Halifax with the advance party of 500 Loyalists from Charleston in December 1782. He was a pioneer, opening new ground in many ways. His ten-year stay in Nova Scotia is recorded in his personal memoirs which were published in Britain in 1793. This remarkable man was not only associated with the founding of the Silver Bluff Baptist Church in South Carolina in 1773 but ten years

later was the founder of the first black Baptist church movement in Nova Scotia. His work in Nova Scotia was carried forward in the nineteenth century by Richard Preston, as well as by many other prominent church leaders, some of whom were privileged to serve the Seaview Baptist Church in Africville.

Besides David George, the eighteenth-century account of black Nova Scotians has a prominent place for the pioneering teachers who, often with limited education themselves, and operating with few resources in depressed conditions, did much to underline the importance of education to raise the standards and strength of the population. Among these teachers were some who also served as preachers, thus marking the beginning of a tradition that continued into the nineteenth and twentieth centuries when preachers and teachers, church and school, worked in tandem to serve a common cause.

Stephen Blucke ran a school in Birchtown supported by the Society for the Propagation of the Gospel. He had thirty-eight pupils in his little school. The conditions were hard; his pupils were in want of food and clothing. He appealed to the Society for relief with which to "cover them, with a suit of clothes, a pair of shoes and a blanket." In his appeal he drew attention to the depressed state of the black community in 1787:

The innumerable hardships, that this new country abounds with, and the very few Opportunitys that the poor blacks enjoy bereaves them of the means for Obtaining more than a scanty pittance of food, and in some families hardly that, which Occasions the poor little objects to be in the pityful situation, they now endure, and must experience still more, if some relief be not handed them....[11]

One of his contemporaries, Boston King, testified to this situation, recounting that many of the poor "were compelled to sell their best gowns for five pounds of flour, in order to support life."[12]

Two other black teachers employed by the Society for the Propagation of the Gospel were notable pioneers: Thomas Brownspriggs taught school in Tracadie and Joseph Leonard in Brindley Town (Digby).

Other teachers of this period included Mrs. Catherine Abernathy who was put in charge of the school at Preston, and Limerick Isaac who was in charge of a school in Halifax. Both were supported by an Anglican charitable institution called the Associates of the Late Dr. Bray. Of Mrs. Abernathy it was reported that she embraced "some Strange religious tenets" and of Isaac it was said that he was an "artful Cunning fellow."[13] These criticisms probably reflect the thinking of the times that Blacks should be subservient to Whites, and should not be independent in thinking or action.

From what we know of the preachers and teachers, the Black Loyalists had pride, ability and initiative. The part played by an activist named Thomas Peters is a good example.

Peters was born in 1741 and worked as a millwright for his master in North Carolina. At the age of twenty-five, he escaped and joined the British army in the American War of Independence holding the rank of sergeant. He was one of hundreds of Blacks who served in a special section called Guides and Pioneers. Peter, his wife and one child, arrived in Port Royal, Annapolis County, in the Loyalist ship, *Joseph*, on May 25, 1784. A leadership role was thrust upon him from the beginning, resulting from the tremendous difficulties faced by the Black Loyalist immigrants. They needed food, shelter, clothing, land, employment and acceptance as new Nova Scotians, but these immigrants found that they were not only voiceless, but they were left to fend for themselves. This situation produced the challenge that Peters accepted. For some eight years, from May 1784 to January 1792, he criss-crossed Nova Scotia and New Brunswick, and eventually went to London, England, in 1790–1791, presenting petitions on behalf of the Black Loyalists of Nova Scotia and New Brunswick, and articulating their grievances with courage and conviction.

What Mathieu da Costa and Barbara Cuffy represent in the seventeenth century in Nova Scotia history, Thomas Peters, Stephen Blucke, David George and many more teachers and preachers represent in the eighteenth century. They exemplify individual abilities and initiative and show that black Nova Scotians have never operated without their own leaders, and their own objectives and expectations. They have left their mark and laid the groundwork for others to build upon.

Of the 3,500 Black Loyalists who came to Nova Scotia between 1782 and 1784, 1,196 left for good after a decade of disappointments, on January 15, 1792. Their departure was a concrete expression of their disillusionment after the promises which had brought them to Nova Scotia. They were recruited by

Rose Fortune was one of many Black Loyalists to come from the United States to Annapolis Royal.

the Sierra Leone Company and they were given land grants in Freetown, Sierra Leone in West Africa.

The more than two thousand that stayed continued to live in the areas of black segregated settlements associated with the Loyalist period. With the passage of time their identities as a distinct Loyalist group merged with the identities of later black immigrants, notably the black refugees of 1813–1816, to constitute what are called "indigenous black Nova Scotians," but are more accurately the founding generation of one of the charter peoples of the province. Their labour, their domestic industry, their market gardening and share-cropping — cultivating the farms of white landowners for a share of the crop harvested — helped the economy of the fledgling colony. The work of individual groups and communities was not lost on succeeding generations.

THE MAROONS

The first black immigrants came to Nova Scotia from the southern colonies and settled all over Nova Scotia. The later group, the Maroons, came from Jamaica and over a four-year period (1796–1800), mainly settled in what is today East Preston, with a small settlement in Boydville, present-day Middle Sackville.

The Maroons occupy a special place in the history of Nova Scotia for a number of reasons. They came involuntarily and virtually in transit, and unlike earlier black immigrants, their coming had nothing to do with events in the United States. They were free Blacks of military bearing, who maintained their independence from colonial rule in Jamaica through a 140-year struggle during which they survived in mountainous hideouts. In 1738 a truce was signed and the Maroons came out of hiding to live side by side with colonized Blacks, as a free community within a larger colonial community. The largest Maroon community was in Trelawny Town in St. James's Parish.

In 1795 the truce broke down. Fierce fighting ensued for some six months before a cease fire was agreed upon with the British rulers of Jamaica. The Maroons laid down their arms on January 1, 1796 only to be accused shortly afterwards of breaking the terms of the cease fire.

As a result, some 550 Maroons were put aboard a ship heading for Nova Scotia. By the time they arrived, war had broken out in Europe, Anglo-French rivalry was being fought out on the high seas and British North America was part of the active war zone. The question of a permanent home for the Maroons of Jamaica was subject to the other priorities of war and security. For the time being, the Maroons could be used in Halifax as labourers or as fighting men in the military — an area in which they were particularly suited. Governor Sir John Wentworth was in favour of keeping the Maroons permanently in Nova Scotia, and the military commander, Prince Edward, saw them as a source of labour for the construction of fortifications on Citadel Hill. In the end, both the governor and the military commander were served by the Maroons, as were the business community of Nova Scotia and the permanent black population of Nova Scotia, all for different reasons.

The finances for maintaining the Maroons in Nova Scotia were provided by the Jamaican government until such time as they were finally and permanently settled. These extended to food, clothing, housing and related expenditures. It was specifically stated in the arrangements for their stay in Nova Scotia that their governance would be in the control of Commissary General, Colonel William Quarrel, a White member of the Jamaica Assembly.

Governor Wentworth chose to ignore these stipulations and went on to assume control over the Maroons. He purchased 1,215 hectares of land with Jamaican government funds to settle them in the Preston area and employed some of the Maroons to work on his own farm in this area. As well, some of them were employed to work at his official residence, Government House, on Barrington Street, Halifax, and on the fortifications on Citadel Hill. He appointed Reverend Benjamin Gerrish Gray to minister to their spiritual needs as well as to their secular education.

The Maroons were pawns in a power struggle between parts of the British Empire as well as between rival factions within Nova Scotia. For their part, they remained largely dissatisfied and disillusioned. They saw their unity eroding, their culture threatened, their future at stake. Having come to Nova Scotia four years after the exodus of 1,196 black Nova Scotians to Sierra Leone, they were no doubt aware of the reasons behind the exodus and of a haven (Sierra Leone) which had a climate similar to that of Jamaica.

In the end, Nova Scotia lost again when, on August 7, 1800, some 551 Maroons left for Sierra Leone on board the *Asia*. This number constituted the majority of the Maroons and their descendants, but not all. A small group remained behind, including some spouses and children. Some families in Nova Scotia after 1800 could trace their links to Maroon antecedents. More significant than the family links were the lessons left behind: the Maroons were free, independent, assertive, proud and strong. They had come from a long line of free men and women accustomed to self-determination. The Maroons did much to destroy common myths about subservience and black inferiority. In this matter, their contribution, though short-lived in terms of time actually spent in Nova Scotia, has had a lasting effect on Nova Scotian society. If black youths today recall slavery with pain, the Black Loyalist experience with disappointment, they invariably identify the Maroon interlude with cohesiveness, dignity and pride.

Above: Many of the Loyalists who had come to Nova Scotia left after years of disappointment were recruited to Freetown, Sierra Leone and given land grants by the Sierra Leone Company.
Right: Jamaican Maroons helped build the Halifax Citadel.

THE BLACK REFUGEES

The one and only organized scheme by which black immigrants were brought to Nova Scotia in the nineteenth century was the coming of the black refugees between 1813 and 1816, bringing to this province some 2,000 persons from the United States.

In many ways this sparked a new era for Blacks. While their emigration from the States was directly due to the circumstances resulting from the American-British War of 1812, they had not been drawn into the conflict as early and as eagerly as the Black Loyalists in the War of Independence of 1775–1782. In the War of 1812, American slaves were kept out of the all-White conflict between the warring nations for two years until the British decided in 1814 to incite rebellion among the slaves. In April 1814 Vice-Admiral Alexander Cochrane issued a proclamation inviting slaves to defect to the British side in return for

slaves, 2,000 of whom were shipped to Nova Scotia.[14]

Their arrival and settlement were beset with problems from the beginning. While Governor John Parr had at least been forewarned of the arrival and settlement of the Black Loyalists in 1782, Governor John Sherbrooke had no such prior warning to prepare for the new refugees. When the advance party of 133 arrived in Halifax in October 1813, there were no funds especially set aside to settle the immigrants, nor was there a plan in place.

This first group comprised 77 men, 29 women and 27 children. The men were listed as labourers, farmers, tradesmen, shoemakers, sawyers and wheelwrights. These skills, typical of the refugees who came later, had been learned and practised in the southern United States.

At the time of their arrival, Nova Scotia was prospering from the fortunes of war — both the French revolutionary war waged in Europe and the American War of 1812–1814 waged along the eastern and southern seaboard of the United States. Unfortunately, however, this prosperity was shortlived as the Peace of Paris in November 1814 put an end to the European hostilities and the Peace of Ghent in December 1814 ended the American War.

Among the first to suffer from the economic downturn were the growing number of destitute black refugees who were neither settled on land grants nor integrated in any way into Nova Scotian society.

It was at the height of this crisis period, in October 1814, that Vice-Admiral Cochrane admitted in a communication to Governor Sherbrooke that the refugee Blacks had crossed over to the British side on the strength of the assurances that their lives would be better and that they would be provided with food, clothing, shelter and a better place to live. The tragedy was that these assurances and promises had not been passed on to the Nova Scotia bureaucracy, nor were they known to the public in Nova Scotia. The various levels of government in London, Bermuda and Halifax failed to act on their good intentions and irreparable damage was done to the independence of the newly-arrived immigrants. Soon, the numbers that lined up for poor relief and for accommodation at the Poor House gave Blacks a bad name, one that persisted for generations.

In light of the exchanges between Cochrane and Sherbrooke in October 1814, it is difficult to understand how Governor Sherbrooke could blame the refugees for their own misfortunes as he did in this despatch to Lord Bathurst, Secretary of State for Colonies in London on October 5, 1814:

I have to state to Your Lordship that though such of them as are industrious can very well maintain themselves as a common labourer here can at this season earn a dollar and a half per day yet the generality of them are so unwilling to work that several of them are absolutely starving owing to their own idleness.[15]

This attitude was inevitably carried into the white population who was never informed about the circumstances and preconditions that brought these refugees to Nova Scotia.

Approximately 1,200 black refugees were landed in Nova Scotia between late 1813 and early 1815 and they were virtually left to fend for themselves. Of this number, 705 were located in the vicinity of Halifax-Dartmouth; 336 in Halifax; 150 in Preston; 72 on the Windsor road; 49 in South East Passage and Cow Bay and 49 on the estate of Rufus Fairbanks at Porters Lake. When the government failed to make good on their guarantees to the new arrivals, individual citizens stepped into the breach out of humanitarian concern. One such man was a Quaker, Seth Coleman, who lived in the Nantucket area of Dartmouth. He had come to the area to carry out business in the whaling industry. He ended up as a champion of the black refugees living in and around Dartmouth.[16]

If the initial batch of 1,200 up to early 1815 was cause enough for concern, the expectation of a further number after March 1815 was viewed with alarm. Governor Sherbrooke admitted as much: "This unexpected importation of so great a number of people of colour for which I was totally unprepared may under the circumstances involve me in difficulty."[17]

Difficulties did come from various quarters: temporary housing at the former military prison on Melville Island was by no means satisfactory. In the three months following March 1815, 727 black refugees were accommodated on Melville Island; an average of 39 were treated daily at the prison hospital, with a fatality list of 76 for this period. This Melville Island "home" for the refugee immigrants lasted for fourteen months in all, providing shelter for about 800 Blacks,

Governor Wentworth had Government House, which would become his official residence, built on Barrington Street in Halifax between 1799 and 1805.

many of whom were reported to be "in a most distressed state afflicted with smallpox, and various other diseases." The mortality rate was reported at just under one-eighth.[18]

This ill-conceived reception made a mockery of the British assurances of freedom and improved living conditions. Governor Sherbrooke's difficulties were compounded by opposition of members of the House of Assembly.

On February 24, 1815, full seventeen months since the first black refugees had arrived, their plight was raised in the House of Assembly. The text of Governor Sherbrooke's message referred to them as persons fleeing "from the calamities of War, and the misery which they were suffering in their native country, to seek an asylum under the protection of the British Government, and have indulged the hope that they will be admitted as free settlers in this Province."[19]

The burden of this message was to liken the black refugees to strangers at the gate, begging for admission, whereas in fact they were brought to the colony on an assisted-emigration scheme. Governor Sherbrooke did not admit to the House of Assembly members that the black refugees had been brought to Nova Scotia as part of Britain's strategy against the Americans in the War of 1812.

Two months later, the members of the House of Assembly gave their response which was clearly an expression of disapproval of this new wave of black immigration to Nova Scotia. They voted £500 to prevent the spread of smallpox among the immigrants and expressed grave concern at the "frequent arrival of Negroes and Mulattoes." They could not understand why public funds should be spent on persons whose "character, principles and habits" had not been previously investigated and, furthermore, they perceived that their presence discouraged white labourers and servants. Blacks, they said, were unsuited by nature to live in Nova Scotia's climate and were a separate class who would never be able to associate with white colonists. For all these reasons, the House of Assembly resolved that steps should be taken to prohibit further black immigration.

The fact that black immigration was not prohibited in 1815 was due to considerations of contemporary British policy and the anti-slavery movement. It was not due to any compromise on Nova Scotia's part. The black refugees had arrived and more were to come. The total of 2,000 were here to stay despite the unwelcome reception.

Governor Sherbrooke advised the British government that the black refugees should be given land grants to settle and cultivate. Mindful of what had happened to the Black Loyalists, he cautioned that they should not be allotted barren land in unfavourable situations. The first such allocation was to settle two hundred families in the Preston area on the very same land which had been acquired earlier to settle the Maroons. Some of the original 1,215 hectares had been sold after the departure of the Maroons in 1800 but most of the land had been repossessed. The settlement plan was for a village made up of four-acre plots which would be occupied through the drawing of lots. An adjoining wooded area of 600 hectares would supply the village with fuel, fencing and building materials. Sherbrooke cautioned that the occupants should have to prove themselves to be worthy settlers. In the meantime, they would be given provisions, implements, construction tools and building boards to make a start. Should they settle down successfully, he argued, there was a market in Halifax for their craft products and their garden produce.

By September 1815, exactly two years after the first group of black refugees arrived in Halifax, the first village comprising 200 lots became a reality in the Preston area. While it was initially recommended that the lots should be no less than four hectares each, the actual grants were smaller because only 740 hectares were made available in an exchange deal with six white property owners. Here and elsewhere the settlers were given licences of occupation and location tickets, not outright ownership of the land they settled on.

In this pioneer village, modest dwellings were erected hastily before the onset of winter. The wood was mainly soft and green. There was hardly any protection against wet or cold. There were no ceilings and, in many cases, no floors. Clothing was scanty and the diet was mainly salted meat and fish. Yet the settlers

were expected to make good on their barely three-hectare lots, grow market produce, fish in the nearby lakes and streams, make shingles, brooms and axe handles. Above all, they were expected to be grateful for the opportunity to settle in this British colony which received them with such hostility and indifference.

Survive they did. During the five winter months, most families cleared up to half a hectare each. By the end of 1816, almost one thousand black refugees — half the total number — settled in the Preston area. This was due to superb community self-help, cohesiveness, faith, and hard work which laid the groundwork for other settlements to follow in what became the black settlements of Halifax County.

The largest of these settlements was Preston where the Black Loyalists had been originally settled in 1784 and where they had continued to live before their exodus to Sierra Leone in 1792. The other black refugee settlements set up between 1815 and 1816 were Hammonds Plains, Windsor Road, Refugee Hill (Halifax), Porters Lake, Beech Hill (later Beechville), Cobequid Road, Prospect Road, Fletchers Lake and Beaver Bank, out of which Lucasville, Cobequid Road and Sackville emerged as time went by, all of which were within a thirty-kilometre radius of Halifax.

Each of these settlements has a history of its own, accounts of men and women who braved the odds to open up new lands and new opportunities while becoming permanent settlers. Before the end of 1816, more than 500 black refugees were settled in Hammonds Plains. The experience of Preston was repeated in Hammonds Plains and in the other settlements.

RESETTLEMENT

While Blacks were establishing themselves in these settlements, there was an ongoing campaign by white Nova Scotians to have them resettled elsewhere in the British Empire.

During the period 1813–16 Vice-Admiral Cochrane's communications to Governor John Sherbrooke made no secret about plans to dispatch black refugees to Nova Scotia. Sherbrooke, in turn, sent dispatches on the matter to the Secretary of State for Colonies, Lord Bathurst. Yet, as late as November 1815, Lord Bathurst informed Governor Sherbrooke that the refugees had been "conveyed to Halifax contrary to the intentions of His Majesty's Government" and asked that steps be

Above: A page from the Book of Negroes, a ledger documenting those who left Manhattan for safe British colonies, including Nova Scotia.

Right: A petition from Black Loyalist Thomas Peters to Lord Grenville, one of the King's principal Secretaries of State, describing the frustrations the Loyalists had over receiving poor land or none at all.

taken to send them to the warmer climate of Trinidad. A few months later, however, Sherbrooke informed Lord Bathurst that the refugees were reluctant to leave in spite of the climate and settlement problems. Then a new governor, Lord Dalhousie, suggested their joining the Black Loyalists and the Maroons in Sierra Leone, or even returning to the United States if a pardon could be worked out. The matter was kept alive by a third governor, Sir James Kempt, in 1820, who used the services of Bishop Inglis to induce the black settlers to emigrate. After years of persuasion, the only success registered was on January 6, 1821 when 81 adults and 14 children, 95 in total, sailed from Halifax to Trinidad.

White hostility and reluctance to accept the black settlers in their midst as permanent fellow citizens led three lieutenant-governors to direct their energies towards relocating the black settlers. While racial intolerance kept alive the idea of resettlement, the settlers were unwilling to leave. Among the reasons was their fear of being re-enslaved.

Whatever their experience with government policy, Blacks who had come as refugees now possessed a piece of land which they had cleared and settled, on which improvements were made, to which they had no title and which they could not sell. Why should they abandon what little they now had?

MOBILITY IN THE BLACK COMMUNITY

Following the arrival of the black refugees, there was considerable mobility within the black communities of Nova Scotia. Individuals and families moved in response to existing situations in matters such as employment, business, markets, property speculation in rare cases, overcrowding, sharecropping, marriages, with the result that peoples of African descent in the province, various immigrant and social groups would meet, mingle and merge from time to time.

There were 765 black slaves in various parts of Nova Scotia in the last quarter of the eighteenth century who were nearly all freed before 1810. Some 2,600 Black Loyalists had remained behind when their counterparts set sail for Sierra Leone in 1792. To these numbers were added the 2,000 black refugees who arrived between 1813–1816.

Thus, in the early years of the nineteenth century when the latest black immigrants were being settled in various places in Halifax County, there were more than 5,000 black people in Nova Scotia, indistinguishable in physical features from the majority black population but with different historical antecedents and experiences. With the passing years, individual and family memories would be the only custodians of these different roots but even these memories became dull with age. In time, who was there to point out the slaves, the Black Loyalists, the black refugees, the Maroons, from one another? And even if the disparate roots could be identified, the individual and separate identities did not matter. For history, there is some point in knowing about one's origin and historical past. For survival, collective associations and strength in numbers are more important than individual identities.

Within ten years of the arrival of the black refugees, the physical landscape began to change as houses sprang up, improvements were made, farms were opened up, and economic activities became heightened. In this setting, progressive individuals began to emerge. One of the original refugee immigrants, Septimus Clarke, who later served the African United Baptist Association for many years, applied for a large grant of land of 100 hectares in 1820. His success in getting fifty hectares was the first record of a black immigrant obtaining an additional grant. This encouraged other Blacks to apply for larger grants ranging from ten hectares to sixty hectares. Forty-two persons were successful. Their names are familiar in the Halifax County up to this day, names such as Bundy, Sparks, Boyd, Clayton, Crawley, Deed, Evans, Grant, Hill, Johnson, Johnston and Smith.[20]

These were the fortunate few who squeezed through before the law was changed in 1827, putting an end to free land grants in Nova Scotia. As overcrowding grew in the newly-settled areas, and with no more free land grants available, the issue of settling and relocating Blacks assumed serious proportions.

The legislature remained adamant in its refusal to make more funds available to ameliorate the lot of the black residents. Lieutenant-Governor Campbell was sympathetic. So were some public-spirited persons like Joseph Howe who supported an appeal to the British government.

The Colonial Secretary agreed to a relaxation of the land laws in 1839. Blacks would be issued land grants elsewhere in the province provided that the cost of relocation was borne by the legislature. Title deeds would not be issued until some time in the future when it was proven that the new settlements were indeed permanent.

It was only in 1842, twenty-seven years later, after the first refugees built their rudimentary houses in 1815, that the Preston settlers were given a general grant covering 730 hectares to replace the temporary and tenuous licences of occupation and tickets of location. By then, they had come to the conclusion that never mind how hard they toiled, there was little they could do with the swampy and barren lands. A group of 107 petitioners asked for titles to their lands so that they could realize value for the improvements made through sales and move to other areas in search

Ships leaving Halifax for Sierra Leone in 1792.

of employment and better land.

The number of Blacks in the Preston area began to decrease: in 1816 it was 924; in 1827 it was 708; in 1838 it was 525 and in 1851 it was as low as 496. The foremost black settlement in Nova Scotia in the nineteenth century was in serious decline.

Individuals and families moved to other places such as Africville, Hammonds Plains and Beechville. Making allowance for spelling variations, the list of family names in the 1847 census throws light on members of the black community living in various parts of Halifax County and elsewhere in Nova Scotia. A few names given alphabetically and in the original spelling illustrate this point: Allen, Beel, Bundy, Carvery, Crawley, Dear, Diggs, Evins, Fletcher, Grant, Henderson, Johnston, Kelly, Lambert, Munro, Pelo, Ranger, Saunders, Taylor, Vass, Wise and Young.[21]

Movements took place in various directions from Preston to Hammonds Plains, to Africville and so on, not necessarily in any particular order. The point simply is that not all families remained in one settlement forever.

In 1851, by which time settlements were in place all over Nova Scotia, the black population numbered 4,908, with females being about 250 more than males. Of this figure, the largest number of 1688 were settled in Halifax County. This included all the black refugee settlements already mentioned. Next came Guysborough County with 603, mostly from Black Loyalist stock; Annapolis had 483; Digby, 454; Yarmouth, 247 and Queen's County had 213. Cape Breton had 238 of which number 162 resided in Sydney. In other places the numbers ranged between 100 and 200. Pictou and Lunenburg had the least with twenty and under.

CHURCH AND SCHOOL

The key institutions of Black communities were church and school. These created an unmistakable bond through the affinity of interests which brought together parents and pupils, teachers and preachers. The legacy of the church and school leaders in the Loyalist era was continued. It is true that by later standards, these custodians of learning and worship were themselves barely literate. They were, however, not unmindful of inadequacies where these existed. In a remarkably frank admission, Boston King, of Loyalist fame, who was a leading preacher during his years in Nova Scotia, went to England after his journey to Sierra Leone, to continue with his education. He wrote in his memoirs:

> *When I first arrived in England, I considered my great ignorance and inability, and that I was among a wise and judicious people, who were greatly my superiors in knowledge and understanding; these reflections had such an effect upon me, that I formed a resolution never to attempt to preach while I stayed in the country ... In the former part of my life I had suffered greatly from the cruelty and injustice of the Whites, which induced me to look upon them, in general as our enemies....* [22]

But Boston King was prevailed upon to preach in England and he was a success.

The story of education for Blacks in Nova Scotia is a long and painful one. From the one-room school in Preston in 1816 to the school in Halifax for black children in 1824, the refugee period in Nova Scotia is replete with problems of funding, finding teachers, keeping schools open, at a time when black teachers were virtually non-existent. The only black teachers in the early years of the nineteenth century were in Tracadie: Thomas Brownspriggs and later, Dempsey Jordan (spelt Jourdan in contemporary reports). In the segregated black settlements, provisions for education were meagre and modest.

As for the black Baptist church, there was no successor to the mantle once worn by David George who left for Africa in 1792. A white Episcopal missionary, John Burton, came to Halifax four months after the departure of David George and worked among black parishioners. He later formed the First Baptist Church at the southeast corner of Barrington and Buckingham streets in Halifax in 1795. Here he ministered to the black refugees of 1813–1816. He is remembered largely for his association with Richard Preston, a remarkable refugee who came to Nova Scotia in 1816, joined Burton's church, served Burton's church, then went to London, England, to pursue his education and seek ordination. Preston returned in 1832, an ordained Baptist pastor, to minister to the newly-formed Cornwallis Street African Baptist Church which he served dutifully until his death in 1861. He founded eleven black Baptist churches between 1832 and 1853 and in 1854 was instrumental in the formation of the African United Baptist Association.

Richard Preston is the nineteenth-century example of an outstanding black Nova Scotian educator, church leader and community activist. He stands as a true colossus in the annals of the history of black Nova Scotians. His work spilled over to the shores of the Bedford Basin where the picturesque Seaview Baptist Church was built, where black residents built their own school, produced their own teachers, mapped out their own memorable destiny. The name Richard Preston is synonymous with the black struggle for identity, survival and progress. His burial site in the Crane Hill Cemetery in East Preston is in the very heart of the nuclear black settlement in Nova Scotia, home to the Black Loyalists, home to the Maroons, home to the black refugees, memorial to the black presence and the black experience in Nova Scotia.

CHAPTER 6

THE SPIRIT LIVES ON:
RECOGNITION, AN APOLOGY AND SETTLEMENT

THE STRUGGLE FOR RECOGNITION

Few people deny that the residents of Africville suffered a terrible injustice. Between 1964 and 1970 they were forcibly removed from their community and relocated in public housing, and their homes and church were razed. After the first edition of this book was published in 1992 the battle for recognition of this injustice, and for proper compensation, continued. Finally, in 2010, many former residents and their descendants were able to put these painful events behind them.

The journey towards closure was long. It was beset by unfulfilled promises and hindered by a stubborn refusal by City officials to admit that the City had done anything wrong. But although the dream of one day rebuilding and resettling Africville — which Africville Genealogy Society (AGS) president Irvine Carvery first demanded of Halifax City Council in 1987 — may have now faded, much else has been achieved.

One of the more devastating blows for many Africville residents had been the loss of their church, bulldozed at the unlikely hour of 3:30 a.m. in 1967. This was the building that Laura Howe, who was relocated from the community with her young family, called Africville's "vocal and spiritual heart." So members of the now-scattered community welcomed an announcement, in 1991, by Deputy Premier Tom McInnis that a replica of Seaview African United Baptist Church would be built. At the same time, he agreed to reroute a road that the Halifax Port Corporation was proposing to run through what was now Seaview Park to improve

truck access to the Fairview Cove container terminal.

In 1992 Martin Luther King III, who was in Halifax to attend the International Gospel Festival, presided over a groundbreaking ceremony on the proposed site of the church reconstruction, but then the project stalled — even though public awareness of Africville was heightened that same year by a national touring exhibition, *Africville: A Spirit that Lives On*, organized by the AGS with Mount Saint Vincent University Art Gallery, the National Film Board of Canada and the Black Cultural Centre of Nova Scotia, and by a half-hour documentary on Africville broadcast by the CBC.

In July 1994, the Province of Nova Scotia announced that it would commit $200,000 to the promised church reconstruction.

That same month, as the annual Africville reunion weekend was drawing to a close, brothers Victor and Eddie Carvery began a protest against the way the City had compensated former members of the Africville community — most families had been paid a paltry $500 or so for the loss of their homes — by setting up a camp in tents and a pair of old trailers in Seaview Park, much to the annoyance of Mayor Walter Fitzgerald. Their camp was set up where the Carvery family home had once stood, at 1833 Barrington Street, and the two men vowed to continue their protest until the City compensated former Africville residents adequately. The City attempted to remove the protesters by introducing a bylaw banning camping in City parks. Concerned that this measure would impact the annual reunion, the AGS was able to get a provision into the bylaw to allow camping during the reunions. Eddie and Victor's response was simple: they moved their protest from Seaview Park to the land where the church and schoolhouse had once stood, just outside the park. Through many other attempts to evict them, the brothers remained.

The situation was exacerbated by a staff report that claimed the City was under no obligation to provide compensation. AGS president Irvine Carvery was highly critical of that report: "It reiterated all of the old racist attitudes shown towards the people of Africville," he recalls.

But by the fall of 1994 Halifax City Council appeared to have had a change of heart about compensation and set up a committee, headed by Mayor Fitzgerald, to look into the matter.

In December of that year the City of Halifax agreed to donate one hectare of land in the Africville Historic Site for the church reconstruction project.

That initiative, however, was short lived. The 1991 McInnis promise to rebuild the church — most likely made in haste to prop up a weak provincial government — had proved hollow and, frustrated by months of inaction and the province's failure to deliver on its promise, the AGS filed a lawsuit against the City for compensation. The City responded by withdrawing its offer of land and steadfastly refused to consider the possibility of individual compensation.

The AGS had received a grant from Heritage Canada to conduct research, and City Hall had agreed to allow the society's researchers very limited access to the City's Africville files for three months. But when that time was up, the AGS had still not completed its examination of the documents, and on March 22, 1995, journalist Stephen Kimber reported in the *Daily News*: "When the deadline came and went last week, some city aldermen moved with unseemly haste to … well, if not declare victory, at least claim that the time for discussion was at an end."

The time for discussion had indeed ended. While the councillors were patting each other on the back for once again sweeping the issue of Africville under the rug, the AGS, along with former residents of Africville and their descendants, following legal advice, served the action on the City of Halifax. It sought damages for the City's failure to provide an Educational Trust

Fund, which had been approved by council in 1994; for its failure to convey land for the construction of the memorial church; and for other long-standing issues of social injustice. It had become clear that the previously independent municipalities of Halifax, Bedford and Dartmouth were about to amalgamate, and the action had to be begun so that the litigation would carry over to the new municipality. In due course, on April 1, 1996, the City of Halifax merged with Bedford and Dartmouth to become the Halifax Regional Municipality (HRM), which assumed all liabilities of the former city.

For the next five years there was little progress at home, but Irvine Carvery was busy telling the Africville story on the world stage. As president of the AGS he attended preparatory meetings — in San Diego, Chile, and in Geneva, Switzerland — that laid the groundwork for the World Conference Against Racism held in Durban, South Africa, in 2001, successfully working to get the issue of Africville placed on the conference agenda, which brought the story to international attention. Following the conference, Canada invited the United Nations special rapporteur on racism, Doudou Diène, to write a report on race relations in Canada. The AGS met with the special rapporteur to present the Africville story, and was able to convince him to come to Africville and walk the grounds that had once been home to Halifax's black community.

Also in 2001, talks did begin behind closed doors between representatives of the former Africville community (in the form of the Africville Genealogy Society) and Halifax Regional Municipality on the question of compensation, which improved relations significantly. Constructive discussions could at last take place in an effort to resolve the outstanding issues and to reach a settlement. And in July 2002 the federal government made a token gesture of acknowledgement by dispatching Heritage Minister Sheila Copps to Halifax to declare the neighbourhood that had once been known as Africville a national historic site. The designation was the result of the efforts of the AGS, which had approached the National Historic Sites board, and was celebrated with a huge ceremony at which Minister Copps unveiled a plaque and presented a design for the site.

But the real turning point, according to Irvine Carvery, came in March 2004, when the United

Nations issued its "Report by Mr. Doudou Diène, Special Rapporteur on contemporary forms of racism, racial discrimination, xenophobia and related intolerance," which urged Ottawa to consider reparations for former Africville residents (as well as for Chinese nationals who had also suffered a serious injustice by being forced to pay a head tax). "That report was the watershed," he told journalist Stephen Kimber. With Ottawa involved, the dialogue recommenced and, Mr. Carvery said, there has been "a very, very positive feeling ever since."

The report's recommendation was not universally well-received by the Halifax public, and provoked a flurry of hostile and ill-informed calls to the *Daily News*'s hotline. Africville residents had already received adequate compensation, claimed some callers, while others blamed the residents for the community's shortcomings — ignoring the fact that the City had denied such basics as sewage service and piped water, yet had used the issue of poor sanitation as one of the reasons for the relocation.

The Genealogy Society dropped its call for individual compensation. It seemed the only way to move matters forward, as HRM flatly refused to negotiate on that issue. "If we wanted that," reflected Irvine Carvery, "we would have had to take them to court. Our legal advisor urged us to negotiate a settlement because the chances of winning in court were very slim."

In 2005, the Africville Genealogy Society completed a three-year strategic plan. Two of its five strategic priorities were: to revive the spirit of Africville by revitalizing the plans to reconstruct Seaview Church, and to celebrate the history of Africville through the creation of an interpretive centre. In June a committee was established with representation from all three levels of government and the AGS to work towards bringing the strategic plan to fulfilment.

In 2006 the Society conducted a feasibility study for construction of the replica church and for the creation of the interpretive centre. AGS was helped with support from HRM, the Nova Scotia Office of African Nova Scotian Affairs, the Nova Scotia Department of Tourism, Culture and Heritage, the Nova Scotia Department of Economic Development, the Department of Canadian Heritage, and the Atlantic Canada Opportunities Agency. A team of consultants was contracted to prepare a study and business plan. The final report was submitted to AGS

and its partners in December.

The study involved extensive consultations with the community, with former Africville residents and their descendants, and with other key stakeholders, such as the Black Cultural Centre for Nova Scotia, the Black Loyalist Heritage Society and the African United Baptists Association. The consultation process included a visioning session with the Board of the Africville Genealogy Society and other community members, interviews with former residents, a public meeting to which former residents and their descendants were invited to provide feedback on the concept, a newsletter to provide updates on the project, and a presentation of the proposed concept at the twenty-third annual Africville picnic.

The consultations identified a number of key issues. For many former Africville residents and their descendants, the deep wounds caused by the destruction of the Africville community had not healed. There was still considerable pain and anger, and former residents reported that this lingering anger remained close to the surface, in part because they did not feel that the issue had been resolved, and they had not had closure. Some said that for them the only way to achieve closure would be through legal action that would return their land, or achieve financial restitution, or both. However, the majority indicated that they were looking simply for an apology.

Overall, those who were consulted supported the concept of a replica church and a separate interpretive centre. A core of former Africville residents and their descendants agreed that the proposed Seaview Church and Africville Interpretive Centre would be important for helping the community to achieve closure, and to heal and prosper. These individuals viewed the centre as a way of continuing to advocate for the people of Africville and to keep the story of their community alive. This community support has remained strong ever since.

There was a shared view that Seaview Church and the Africville Interpretive Centre could play a number of important roles, such as facilitating healing by rebuilding community connections; ensuring the story of Africville will be known to future generations; and encouraging learning, exploration and contemplation of issues that are of relevance to the community.

Following completion of the 2006 feasibility study and business plan, the AGS and all three levels of government worked to secure the support necessary to implement the church/interpretive centre project. The interpretive centre was to be built first, then the church.

The proposed site consisted of just over one hectare of land, bounded by Bedford Basin to the west, the Africville Historic Site to the north, Africville Road (formerly Barrington Street and Service Road) to the east and the City of Halifax Works Division Yard to the south. A shallow ditch divided the property from the Works Division Yard. More than half of the lot consisted of filled land that did not exist for much of the period that the original Seaview Church stood nearby.

In view of some of the physical insults that had been inflicted upon the community — such as the siting of the city dump close by Africville in the mid-1950s — it was necessary to carry out an environmental assessment and a health and human risk assessment of the proposed site. Fortunately, nothing was found that constituted a human health risk.

Geotechnical testing, however, indicated that much of the site, being on fill, would not be able to support a building. This, combined with the fact that the Service Road now cuts through where the old church stood, meant that it would not be possible to construct the new church in exactly the same location as the original.

Every year, during the last week of July, the AGS holds the Africville reunion and picnic in Seaview Park, at the foot of the A. Murray MacKay Bridge, where the community of Africville once stood. On the Friday, the celebration typically kicks off with a dance featuring performances by local talent. On Saturday, there are games for the children and a food court. Sundays are reserved for religious and musical events. The picnic typically attracts upwards of one thousand people, many from the community at large, but the 2008 event, the twenty-fifth, was attended by more than fifteen hundred people from all parts of Canada, the US and beyond. The Paramount Chief from Ghana addressed the gala gathering. Two other events also made the summer of 2008 especially memorable for Nova Scotia's black community: the visit of the Freedom Schooner *Amistad* to Halifax and a performance of Africville descendant Joe Sealy's *Africville Suite* at the city's Neptune Theatre.

On June 15, 2009, the Rev. Jesse Jackson was invited to Halifax by the Canadian branch of the National Alliance of Black School Educators to speak to their group and was presented with a book about Africville by Irvine Carvery in his capacity as chair of the Halifax Regional Municipality School Board. The 2009 annual reunion and picnic was notable for a small but significant acknowledgement from HRM: the road leading to Seaview Park and to the Fairview container terminal would be renamed Africville Road. This move was welcomed by Irvine Carvery. "The name Africville speaks to the former residents and their descendants about home, a place where their ancestors celebrated life in a close-knit community that remains an indelible part of the city's history. The renaming of the road that once led to Africville will allow generations to come to feel a tangible connection to their roots and a sense of belonging," he said.

In the fall of 2009 the AGS, in consultation with federal, provincial and municipal government representatives, decided that it would be better to move forward with the reconstruction of Seaview Church as the first phase of the project, rather than the second. The AGS and the Black Business Initiative contracted a team of consultants to update the 2006 Business Plan, to develop more detailed plans for its implementation and to provide advisory services in the establishment of the Africville Heritage Trust Society, the governing body intended to own and operate both the Seaview Church and the Africville Interpretive Centre.

AN APOLOGY AND SETTLEMENT

We apologize. These were the words that the people of Africville had waited almost half a century to hear. Finally, on Wednesday, February 24, 2010, Mayor Peter Kelly, on behalf of Halifax Regional Council and Halifax Regional Municipality, stood before an assembled crowd, which included many former Africville residents and their descendants, and delivered a formal apology for the loss of their historic community.

"On behalf of the Halifax Regional Municipality," he said,

I apologize to the former Africville residents and their descendants for what they have endured for almost fifty years, ever since the loss of their community that had stood on the shores of Bedford Basin for more than one hundred fifty years.

You lost your houses, your church, all of the places

where you gathered with family and friends to mark the milestones of your lives.

For all that, we apologize.

We apologize to the community elders, including those who did not live to see this day, for the pain and loss of dignity you experienced.

We apologize to the generations who followed, for the deep wounds you have inherited and the way your lives were disrupted by the disappearance of your community.

We apologize for the heartache experienced at the loss of the Seaview United Baptist Church, the spiritual heart of the community, removed in the middle of the night. We acknowledge the tremendous importance the church had, both for the congregation and the community as a whole.

We realize words cannot undo what has been done, but we are profoundly sorry and apologize to all the former residents and their descendants.

The repercussions of what happened in Africville linger to this day. They haunt us in the form of lost opportunities for young people who were never nurtured in the rich traditions, culture and heritage of Africville.

They play out in lingering feelings of hurt and distrust, emotions that this municipality continues to work hard with the African Nova Scotian community to overcome.

For all the distressing consequences, we apologize.

Our history cannot be rewritten but, thankfully, the future is a blank page and, starting today, we hold the pen with which we can write a shared tomorrow.

It is in that spirit of respect and reconciliation that we ask your forgiveness.

Mayor Kelly then announced the terms of an agreement between the municipality and the Africville Genealogy Society to commemorate the historic Africville community, an agreement that he said was designed to honour the past, to take action in the present and to plan for community-based improvements for the future:

• HRM was to contribute $3 million toward the reconstruction and operation of the Seaview African United Baptist Church to serve as a memorial to Africville. Funds in the Africville Trust account and the Self Insurance Reserve would be transferred to

a new organization to be known as the Africville Heritage Trust, established specifically to operate the replica Seaview African United Baptist Church and the Interpretive Centre. The Founding Board of Directors for the Africville Heritage Trust would include six representatives from the Africville community, including representation from the Africville Genealogy Society, as well as five external members, chosen for their expertise in the areas of work and challenge that the new organization would face, and as many as three non-voting positions to be filled by representatives from government agencies, to ensure continuity and ongoing dialogue.

• The municipality would transfer 2.5 acres of land adjoining Seaview Park to a new organization, the Africville Heritage Trust Board.

• A park maintenance agreement would be established between the Africville Heritage Trust and HRM for the lands known as Seaview Park (HRM would still own the land).

• Seaview Park would be officially renamed Africville.

• An African-Nova Scotian Affairs office or function was to be established within HRM, to enable the AGS to better engage with the municipality's African community.

For the Africville Genealogy Society, which represented former residents and their descendants, and which had long sought a fitting recognition of Africville and a way to ensure its history remained a significant part of the fabric of the municipality, the apology and settlement were the culmination of many years of hard work.

"This announcement, with its heartfelt apology, is welcomed by the people of Africville," said society president Irvine Carvery. "Today, as we open the door to tomorrow, we do it on the sacrifices and struggles of those who came before us. This is truly a new beginning for Africville."

Not everyone was satisfied with the settlement, and the issue of individual compensation — notable by its absence from the HRM offer — still rankled with some former residents and their descendants. "Our fight has just started," announced Eddie Carvery, after hearing

Mayor Kelly's apology. He remained sceptical about the municipality's intentions. "We'll fight for our individual compensation, we'll fight for a public inquiry," he said. "Thank you for the apology. Accepted. Two more to go." Throughout the long years of their protest, he and his brother Victor received much moral support from both black and white communities. In September 2009 they were joined in their protest by their cousin Nelson Carvery, who is the son of Aaron (Pa) Carvery, Africville's very last resident.

In addition, a handful of former residents and their descendants questioned the legality of the compensation package on the grounds that Irvine Carvery and the AGS had no mandate to negotiate directly with the City. The AGS, however, had sought legal opinion on the matter. "This clearly stated that we were within our legal rights to negotiate a settlement," says Carvery. By July 2010 the AGS was in the process of removing from the courts the litigation that it had started against HRM in March of 1995.

Perhaps the Reverend Rhonda Britten most accurately summed up the feelings of the majority of those present at Mayor Kelly's apology and the announcement of the settlement. "I know that there are some among us who are wounded," she said, "and some among us who bear those scars. But, in spite of all of that, the victory has been won. We must forgive and must push forward."

RISING FROM THE ASHES

A few weeks after the public apology, in May 2010, with funding from the Atlantic Canada Opportunities Agency, the update of the 2006 feasibility study and business plan was made public.

The first phase was to be the construction and opening of the replica of the Seaview African United Baptist Church that used to stand at the heart of the Africville community. Plans were for the building to house an introductory exhibit on the history of Africville, with ground to be broken in 2010 and the official opening to be at the Africville reunion in July 2011. The second phase would involve the development of a larger interpretive centre that would tell the full story of Africville and provide space for educational programs and gatherings. The opening of the interpretive centre was projected for 2014.

Exhibits for the church and interpretive centre were to have three major themes: *Building a Community:* *Life in Africville*; *The Community Uprooted*; and *The Community Lives On: Africville's Legacy*. In addition, a variety of programs would be offered for school groups and for youth, as well as adult education and outreach programs. The space would also be a community meeting space for special events, such as weddings.

It would be a fitting memorial to the community that *was* Africville, and *is* Africville once again. The spirit lives on.

PHOTO CREDITS

The editors and publishers acknowledge and thank the following copyright holders and archives for the use of photographs reproduced in this book.

PRELIMINARY PAGES

5 — Rosella Carvery and Deborah Lawrence, 1957 — Collection of Evelyn Lawrence; 6 — Ted Grant, National Archives of Canada, accession #1981-181 (henceforth cited as Ted Grant), A; 8 — Canada's Visual History, National Film Board.

CHAPTER 1

9 — Ted Grant, 114; 10-11 — Ted Grant, 120; 11 (right) — Ted Grant, 55; 12 — Albert Lee; 13 (top) —Halifax Herald Ltd.; 14 — CMHC/National Archives of Canada/PA-170731; 16-17 — Ted Grant, 148; 17 (right) — Ted Grant,140; 26-27 — Ted Grant,18; 26 (right) — Halifax Herald Ltd; 20 (top) — Ted Grant, 106; 24 — Ted Grant, 136; 25 — Bob Brooks collection, Public Archives of Nova Scotia (PANS) (henceforth cited as Bob Brooks/PANS); 26 — Ted Grant, 30; 27 (bottom) — Ted Grant,179; 28-29 — Halifax Police Department Museum; 30 — Ted Grant, 87.

CHAPTER 2

36 — Halifax Herald Ltd.; 37 — CMHC/National Archives of Canada/PA-170739; 39 (bottom) — Photograph collection, Public Archives of Nova Scotia (henceforth cited as PANS); 40 (top) — Jessie Kane; 40 (bottom) — Ruth Brown Johnson; 42 — Ruth Brown Johnson; 45 (top) — Black Cultural Centre; 45 (bottom) — Ruth Brown Johnson; 46-47 — Clara Adams; 47 (right) — Ruth Brown Johnson; 48 — Ray and Evelyn Lawrence; 50-51 — CMHC/National Archives of Canada/PA-170741; 52 — Black Cultural Centre; 53 — PANS; 54 — Ted Grant — 163; 55 — National Archives of Canada.

CHAPTER 3

57 — Ted Grant, 188; 60 (top and bottom) — Bob Brooks/PANS; 61, 62, 63 — Photograph collection, PANS; 64 — Bob Brooks/PANS; 65 — Photograph collection, PANS; 66-67 — Bob Brooks/PANS; 67 — Photograph collection, PANS; 71 — Photograph collection, PANS; 72 (top) — Ted Grant, 211; 72 (left) — Ted Grant, 212; 73 (top) — Ted Grant, 201; 73 (right) — Ted Grant, 207; 75 — Halifax Herald Ltd.; 77 — Photograph collection, PANS.

CHAPTER 4

79 — Stanley Carvery; 81 (top) — Halifax Herald; 82 (right and left) — Keith Vaughan; 86 — Ardith Pye; 87, 88, 90, 91, 93, 95, 96, 97, 98, 99, 100, 102, 103, 104 — Donna James; 92 (left) — Keith Vaughan.

CHAPTER 5

106 — Library and Archives Canada/Credit: W. Booth/ W.H. Coverdale Collection of Canadiana/C-040162; 107 — Library and Archives Canada/Credit: Robert Petley/Robert Petley collection/C-003558; 108 — Tracy W. McGregor Library of American History, Special Collections, University of Virginia Library; 109 — Nova Scotia Archives and Records Management Map Collection 239-1798; 111 — Nova Scotia Archives and Records Management Art Collection, acc. no. 1979-147/56; 113 (top) — Royal Geographical Society, London, UK/The Bridgeman Art Library; 113 (right) — Schomburg Center/Art Resource, NY; 115 — Library and Archives Canada/Credit: John Elliott Woolford (1778-1866)/John Elliott Woolford Collection/C-003558; 117 (top) — The National Archives, UK; 117 (right) — TNA(PRO)F04-1f421, The National Archives, UK; 119 — Maritime Museum of the Atlantic, m2008.38.1.

FRONT COVER

(top right and bottom left): Ted Grant.

BACK COVER

(top middle and bottom left): Ted Grant.

ENDNOTES

1   Originally published in the exhibit catalogue entitled, *Africville, A Spirit That Lives On* (1989).

2   With few exceptions all quotations used in Chapters 2 and 3 have been taken from Donald H. Clairmont and Dennis W. Magill, *The Africville Relocation Report, Volumes 1 and 2* (Halifax: The Institute of Public Affairs, Dalhousie University, 1971, 1973). For a more detailed and wider reaching assessment of the Africville Relocation the reader is referred to the book by the same authors, *Africville: The Life and Death of a Canadian Black Community* (Toronto: Canadian Scholars' Press, revised edition, 1987).

3   Dixon is widely credited as the driving force behind the Africville Genealogy Society. By the time "Africville: A Spirit That Lives On" exhibition and conference finally became a reality, however, she had developed cancer and was too ill to participate actively in most of the activities surrounding the event. She did speak briefly at the opening of the exhibition. She died a few weeks later.

4   Besides Carvery and Deborah Dixon, Brenda Steed-Ross and Irvine's cousin, Stan Carvery, have also served terms as presidents of the society.

5   The transcripts included here have been condensed and adapted from the conference proceedings.

6   John N. Grant, *The Immigration and Settlement of the Black Refugees of the War of 1812 in Nova Scotia and New Brunswick* (Dartmouth, Nova Scotia: Black Cultural Association, 1990), 1–4.Bridglal Pachai, *Beneath the Clouds of the Promised Land. The Survival of Nova Scotia's Blacks, Vol. I, 1600–1800* (Halifax: Black Educators Association, 1987), 39–41.

7   R. A. McLean, "The Scots-Hector's Cargo," in Douglas F. Campbell, *Banked Fires — The Ethnics of Nova Scotia* (Port Credit, Ontario: The Scribblers' Press, 1979), 107.

8   Dorrie Phillips, "Early Years of the Black Loyalists" in *Loyalists in Nova Scotia*, ed. Donald Wetmore and Lester B. Sellick (Hantsport, Nova Scotia: Lancelot Press, 1983), 71.

9   James Walker, *The Black Loyalists. The Search for a Promised Land in Nova Scotia and Sierra Leone, 1783–1870* (New York: Africana Publishing Company, 1976).

10 Pachai, *Beneath the Clouds,* 47.

11 Ethel Gibson Wilson, *The Loyal Blacks* (New York: G. P. Putnam & Sons, 1976), 91.

12 Boston King, "Memoirs," *The Methodist Magazine*, May, 1798 (London: Baptist Annual Register).

13 Gibson Wilson, *Loyal Blacks*, 77.

14 Grant, *Immigration and Settlement*; John N. Grant, "Chesapeake blacks who immigrated to New Brunswick, 1815," *National Genealogical Society Quarterly*, Vol. 60, Number 3 (September 1972); John N. Grant, "Black Immigrants into Nova Scotia," *The Journal of Negro History*, Vol. LVIII, No. 3 (July 1973); John N. Grant, "Early Blacks of Nova Scotia," *Journal of Education*, Vol 5, No. 1 (Fall 1977).

15 CO. 217/93. Nova Scotia Archives & Records Management.

16 Pachai, *Beneath the Clouds*

17 Grant, "Black Immigrants," 268.

18 Ibid., 269–70.

19 C. B. Fergusson, *A Documentary Study of the Establishment of the Negroes in Nova Scotia Between the War of 1812 and the Winning of Responsible Government* (Halifax: Public Archives of Nova Scotia, 1948), 17.

20 Ibid., 45–46

21 Terrence M. Punch, "The Black Population of Preston, Halifax County, in 1847," *Sources for Research*, PANS, Vol. IV/1, 39.

22 King, "Memoirs," 283.